Stories Told Under The Sycamore Tree

A gift for St. Mark's United Methodist Church from Sam & Jeanita Hahn

Lessons
From
Bible
Plants

Samuel J. Hahn

Illustrated by
Scott Patton

CSS Publishing Company, Inc., Lima, Ohio

STORIES TOLD UNDER THE SYCAMORE TREE

Copyright © 2003 by
CSS Publishing Company, Inc.
Lima, Ohio

Library of Congress Cataloging-in-Publication Data

Hahn, Samuel J., 1930-
    Stories told under the sycamore tree : Bible plant object lessons / Samuel J. Hahn ; illustrated by Scott Patton.
        p. cm.
    Includes index.
    Summary: Fifty-two devotions based on plants named in the Bible.
    ISBN 0-7880-1972-4 (pbk.)
    1. Plants in the Bible—Juvenile literature. 2. Christian children—Prayer-books and devotions—English. [1. Plants in the Bible. 2. Prayer books and devotions.] I. Patton, Scott, ill. II. Title.
    BS665.H34 2003
    220.8'58—dc21
                                                                    2003003528

For more information about CSS Publishing Company resources, visit our website at www.csspub.com or e-mail us at custserv@csspub.com or call (800) 241-4056.

ISBN 0-7880-1972-4   PRINTED IN U.S.A.

Author's Dedication

I would like to dedicate this book to my children, Eunice, Jonathan, and Deborah; my grandchildren, Benjamin, Matthew, and Adam; my charming wife Juanita; and in memory of my parents, Henry and Carrie Hahn.

Each of these people has touched and blessed my life in a significant way!

Above all, this is dedicated to God, to his glory and his purpose!

— *Samuel J. Hahn*

Artist's Dedication

*When Sam and I were mulling over the idea for a follow-up to **Learning From The Lizard**, it was a dear friend, Marvel Clark, who suggested the theme of Bible plants, which in these pages becomes reality. Marvel tends an extensive wildflower park near Perry, Iowa. Her knowledge of plants is surpassed only by her love of God's creation. Thanks, Marvel!*

I would like to thank my wife Deb for her unwavering support on this project. Her encouragement has meant more than words can say. I dedicate the art in this book to her and our daughter Madaline who bring so much love and joy into my life.

Lastly, I dedicate this art with a grateful heart to our Heavenly Father, the source of all gifts, who continually makes all things possible. This book is testimony to that.

— *Scott Patton*

Acknowledgments

I want to acknowledge a helpful comment from a friend who wrote after reading *Learning From The Lizard*: "This is a beautifully written and illustrated book. Thank you for sharing it."

Two books have been very helpful in writing this book: *All the Plants of the Bible* by Winifred Walker and *The Daily Study Bible*, a scholarly and treasured commentary on the New Testament by William Barclay.

For this book and my earlier book, Bishop Reuben Job, Bishop Wayne Clymer, and Mrs. Ruth Stafford Peale have given helpful and much appreciated support! My wife Juanita has provided helpful proofreading and advice, and our daughter Deborah has graciously helped type the manuscript.

Most obviously, I acknowledge the colorfully and beautifully pictured artwork of each plant by nature artist Scott Patton.

Table Of Contents

VI. Plants For Food

VII. Plants For Medicine

VIII. Plants For Common Uses

Preface

Coming from a farm background, I have always been fascinated with the biblical references to plants and animals. In an earlier book, *Learning From The Lizard*, I wrote about 25 animals and birds that are a part of the biblical writings. In this book dealing with the Bible flora, we have found significant botanical material to portray accurately each plant included.

Nature artist, Scott Patton, who has won many awards for his artwork of nature, skillfully illustrated *Learning From The Lizard* with black and white drawings. For this book he has used color, artistically portraying the splendor of these plants.

I believe you will find these stories useful for sermon preparation, for devotions during men's, women's, or youth groups, as well as for children's sermons. It's a spiritual resource you may refer to again and again.

> *Jesus said, "Consider the lilies, how they grow: they neither toil nor spin; yet I tell you, even Solomon in all his glory was not clothed like one of these. But if God so clothes the grass of the field, which is alive today and tomorrow is thrown into the oven, how much more will he clothe you...?"* — Luke 12:27-28 (NRSV)

Over 120 different species of plants are referred to in the Bible, and from each of these we can learn a lesson. I have chosen to include 52 of the more notable ones in this book. There is one colorful picture and theme for each week of the year, or for 52 days of devotions.

I vividly remember the lilies of the field from a spring-time trip I took to Palestine. It is not a true lily, but, as is pictured in this book, it is a scarlet anemone, and some of the fields were carpeted with them. When our tour bus stopped so we could take some pictures, a boy about eight years old came running with a handful of the flowers hoping to sell them for an "American dollar." His disappointment was very obvious when I did not accept his offer. If I had it to do over, I would gladly have given him an "American dollar," with the grateful comment, "Yes, these are a gift from God freely given to all, and I thank you for sharing God's gift of charming flowers with me!"

This book has several purposes. First, I hope to direct readers to make diligent use of the Bible and to have a creative guide for devotions. Second, I have used these thoughts as a source for children's stories. Third, I pray that the message and the love of Jesus will be more alive for each reader. Finally, I trust that we all can have a better understanding of the wonders of God's creation.

With extensive research, I have tried to be scientifically accurate with names, uses, and lessons that come from these plants. The artist has carefully studied each plant presented, accurately portraying each plant, tree, or blossom. I pray that readers will feast their eyes and thoughts on this material.

Foreword

Writing *Stories Told Under The Sycamore Tree* has helped answer some questions for me. The Scriptures and poets have spoken of Jesus as "The Lily of the Valley," and "The Rose of Sharon." What did these plants look like? It was fascinating to find out that neither plant is what I had imagined; not a lily or a rose as we know them.

Across the street from where my wife and I live are some sycamore trees that are always undressing, in terms of shedding leaves, and shedding a layer of bark. The Bible speaks of Amos as a "dresser of sycamore trees." Again we find out that it is a completely different species of tree. I am confident that the colorful picturing of these plants by Scott Patton will give a greater understanding of the scripture and the powerful message it has for each of us. I will be pleased with the purpose of this book, if it helps even a few come to a better acceptance of the Bible as God's Word for us today, and an acceptance of His Word for every generation.

Whatever obstacles, challenges, or burdens you may be facing in life, here are words of assurance: "Be like a tree" (Psalm 1); "Consider the lilies" (Matthew 6:28).

Read these stories to your children, or better yet, have them read these stories to you. Give them some paper and crayons, and challenge them to make a Bible flower garden or drawings of trees.

We live at a time of extraordinary interest in nature. A time when these stories are sought after and enjoyed. Share the stories and share the book as a gift.

Apple

Golden And Tempting

*A word fitly spoken is like **apples** of gold in a setting of silver.* — Proverbs 25:11 (NRSV)

One of the best known stories in the Bible is about Eve being tempted by Satan to eat the delicious fruit of the apple tree (Genesis 3:1-13). What could be more tempting than a luscious, juicy, red apple? But the Bible does not say it was an apple. What was the tree that helped to set in motion the sin and disobedience of humanity? Today most authorities agree that whatever fruit it was, it most certainly was not an apple.

Apples as we know them have been developed within the last 200 years. Most botanists agree that the apple did not even exist in the Near East in ancient times. And if there was an apple, it would have been a little sour crab of poor quality. Botanical classification was unknown before the seventh century, and up until that time many kinds of fruit were known as "apples." Tomatoes were known as "love apples" and dates as "finger apples." The pomegranate was even known as the "apple of Carthage." On the other hand, "apples of gold," referring to the apricot, were in existence and, with proper care, produced deliciously sweet and satisfying fruit.

The climate of Palestine is ideal for apricots. In the highlands and lowlands, along the Mediterranean Sea or Jordan River, the apricot flourishes and produces crops of abundance. Some biblical scholars express with conviction that, for them, there is no doubt that the apple in the Bible is actually the apricot. "As an apple tree among the trees of the wood, so is my beloved among young men. With great delight I sat in his shadow, and his fruit was sweet to my taste" (Song of Solomon 2:3 NRSV).

The tree grows to thirty feet in height. Early blossoms are pale rose in color with a rich carmine center. The branches bearing the fruit, trunk, and boughs are rough and gnarled. The fruit is very

Scott Patton

aromatic and delicious. Each apricot has a large seed from which prussic acid, used as a medicine or perfume, is made.

Not only was the tree good for food, but it also was "a delight to the eyes," and Eve, then Adam, disobeyed. Perhaps the worst sin was in terms of the temptation to "be like God" (Genesis 3:5).

Lessons From The Apple

The verse from Proverbs 25:11 talks about the value of the right words, at the right time. Such words are like gold in silver settings. Use your words today to encourage, support, and comfort those you meet, maybe even to bring laughter to a heavy heart. If your words have been heavy and harsh, have the courage to seek forgiveness.

Prayer

Dear Lord, today I am thinking about words. Thank you for words I have heard that brought help, healing, joy, or laughter. I want my words to be words of love and restoration.

Direct me, by the guidance of your Holy Spirit, to share in the task of lifting others with your love. Please, Lord Jesus, carry me through the heaviest storms of life, leaving only your steadfast footprints, even when I feel forsaken.

We pray in the holy and healing name of Jesus. Amen!

Fig

Fable Or Fact?

*The Lord showed me two baskets of **figs** placed in front
of the temple ... The first basket contained good **figs**,
those that ripen early; the other one contained bad **figs**,
too bad to eat....*
*So the Lord said to me, "I, the Lord, the God of
Israel, consider that the people who were taken away
to Babylonia are like these good **figs**, and I will treat
them with kindness ... I will give them the desire to know
that I am the Lord. Then they will be my people, and I
will be their God, because they will return to me with
all their heart."*

— Jeremiah 24:1, 2, 4-5, 7 (TEV)

The fig is a very prominent food for the people of Palestine. In
the Bible, "fig" is used 57 times. Fig is the first of the fruits mentioned in the Bible. The leaves were used to make a covering for
Adam and Eve.

"... and they sewed fig leaves together, and made themselves
aprons" (Genesis 3:7). After eating from the "tree of knowledge,"
they felt naked and guilty.

The large, tough leaves of the fig tree would be suitable for
clothing. In some places the leaves are used to make baskets, dishes,
and umbrellas. The leaves are also used to wrap food for market
and for a variety of other uses.

Since the dawn of civilization, the fig has been an important
source of food. It normally bears two crops: one early, appearing
before the leaves and maturing in late June. The second crop is
produced on new branches and matures in late August.

The fig's flowers are inconspicuous. They are enclosed in a
large hollow receptacle. The tiny fig wasp is crucial for the production of the flower's tasty fruit seeds. This wasp, only one-eighth
of an inch long, enters and fertilizes the hidden blossoms. Conse-
quently, when a large, tasty variety of fig was introduced to the

Scott Potter

United States, it produced tasteless, tiny figs. Then it was discovered that the fig wasp was a vital part of fruit production. The wasp was introduced to the area of the fig trees, and soon the new plants were producing large, luscious figs. The tree itself is ideal for picking, being no more than 25 feet tall with spreading branches.

In Palestine, figs are usually eaten fresh. They are dried and threaded on long strings if taken on journeys. 1 Samuel 25:18 mentions "cakes of figs," prepared for eating while traveling. Fig bars are one of the delicious fig foods available here in the United States.

A significant Bible passage mentioning figs:

> *The Lord your God is bringing you into a fertile land — a land that has rivers and springs, and underground streams gushing out into the valleys and hills; a land that produces wheat and barley, grapes, figs, pomegranates, olives, and honey.*
> — Deuteronomy 8:7-8 (TEV)

At the height of the glory of Israel, 1 Kings 4:25 (TEV) says: "... The people throughout Judah and Israel lived in safety, each family with its own grapevines and fig trees."

Without figs, some of the pages of history would have been dramatically changed.

Lessons From The Fig

Nature shows an amazing interdependence. What if someone had developed a pesticide to destroy the pesky little fig wasp, that can sting if aggravated? Misunderstanding nature's ways could have wiped out the value of the fig! It's a fact, not a fable, that the fig can be easily dried, stored, and eaten. They have a long, usable life as food without special preservation. Figs provide a powerful lesson about God's ultimate plan using a tree dependent on a wasp. How much do we depend on God's love?

Prayer

Gracious God, we see how you make provision for people in all situations. After their disobedience, Adam and Eve found the fig tree as a provision for clothing.

We now have food and clothing supplies from all parts of the world. Please help us be aware of all places producing food, fiber, and manufactured goods. Help these places have adequate wages and adequate living conditions. Thank you for the fig. Guide us with compassion for all people who help produce our expanding supply of food. Amen!

Grape Vine

A Vine For Joy

*"I am the true **vine**, and my Father is the **vine** grower*
... Abide in me as I abide in you. Just as the branch
*cannot bear fruit by itself unless it abides in the **vine**,*
*neither can you unless you abide in me. I am the **vine**,*
you are the branches ... I have said these things to you
so that my joy may be in you, and that your joy may be
complete." — John 15:1, 4,11 (NRSV)

Some people try to get joy out of a bottle of wine, and even the Psalmist says: "... he can grow his crops and produce wine to make him happy, olive oil to make him cheerful, and bread to give him strength" (Psalm 104:14-15 TEV).

But the transforming truth is that the real source of joy is our relationship with God. We must abide in him.

The story of the grape vine, as related in the Bible, is an extensive and fascinating story. The word *vine* and words containing *vine* are used 203 times. The word *wine* and words containing *wine* are used about 230 times. *Grape* in various forms is used 48 times. The first reference in the Bible is in Genesis 9, where Noah planted a vineyard after leaving the ark. The growing of grapes, known as viticulture, is one of the oldest forms of agriculture. The vine was no doubt cultivated before the flood, and growing grapes became one of the major occupations of the Mediterranean world.

Isaiah provides a detailed description of the planting of a vineyard (Isaiah 5:1-6).

> *... on a very fertile hill. He dug the soil and cleared it of*
> *stones; he planted the finest vines. He built a tower to*
> *guard them, dug a pit for treading the grapes.*
> — Isaiah 5:2 (TEV)

All of the larger vineyards had a stone fence and a stone watchtower. The owner might live in the tower when the grapes were

Scott Patton

ripe, or he would hire a guard. The watchtower often had a winepress at the floor level, where barefooted individuals could walk amongst the grapes and press out the wine. During the vintage season, the guardians lived in the watchtower.

Pruning was an important part of viticulture. After the grapes were formed, the nonbearing branches would be pruned off, providing more nourishment to the forming grapes. Pruning, severely cutting the vines back, was also done after harvest or before leaves appeared in the spring.

In Palestine grapes begin to ripen toward the end of July, but the harvest doesn't take place until August or September. The early grapes tended to be sour and set the teeth on edge (Jeremiah 31:29-30; Ezekiel 18:2). The ripe grapes could be eaten in their natural state, dried and made into raisins, boiled down into a thick grape syrup, or made into wine. There are some interesting rules in the Old Testament about vineyards. Grapes not harvested the first time over were to be left for the poor, widows, orphans, or foreigners (Leviticus 19:10; Deuteronomy 24:21). Vineyards were to lie fallow for the Sabbath, every seventh year (Exodus 23:10-11; Leviticus 25:3-5). Most unusual was the stipulation that he who had just planted a vineyard was to be exempt from military service (Deuteronomy 20:6).

One reason the spies sent to the Holy Land by Moses were so impressed with the large grapes was that in Egypt the grapes were much smaller and of inferior quality. Throughout the Old Testament, the abundance of vineyards is evidence of God's favor (Hosea 2:15).

In the New Testament, Jesus often makes reference to vineyards. In one reference, he compares the kingdom of heaven to a vineyard. The owner hired workers throughout the day. Surprisingly, those hired toward the close of the day received the same wage as those who had worked all day (Matthew 20:1-16). Also Jesus tells about a son who first refuses to work for his father in the vineyard. He then has a change of heart and goes to work (Matthew 21:28-32). Matthew 21:33-43 also tells the parable of the landowner, representing God, who rented his vineyard to tenants, representing the Jews. When the owner attempts to collect the harvest, the tenants refuse payment even to the extent of killing the son, representing Jesus. Jesus concluded: "And so I tell you, the kingdom of God will be taken away from you and given to a people who will produce the proper fruits" (Matthew 21:43 TEV). In John 15 (some of the verses are quoted at the beginning of this story), Jesus uses the vine for the basis of one of his marvelous teachings. He is the vine and we are the branches, eminently dependent on him. Apart from him we bear no fruit, and are cast out, even burned.

Lessons From The Grape Vine

If left to their own wild and straggly growth, grape vines are nearly worthless. They must be diligently cultivated, pruned, and cared for. If given dedicated care, the vines will produce choice, delicious fruit. Jesus gave an unsurpassed teaching as he said: "As the branch cannot bear fruit by itself, unless it abides in the vine, neither can you, unless you abide in me" (John 15:4 NRSV).

Prayer

Gracious Lord Jesus,
Truly you are the vine,
The source of life and nourishment.
You have called us to be branches,
To receive from you continual
Nourishment and invigorating strength.
Lord Jesus, we want to bear fruit for you.
We want to be so close to the vine,
That your Holy Spirit will produce
Love, joy, peace, patience, and kindness.
Forgive us for those times when we have
Failed, because we were not united to you.
We must face painful pruning but
Avoid drying up as cast-off branches.
As we abide in you, we know fruit, including real joy,
Will be produced.
We are committed to receive

23

And follow your commandment
To love one another.
So may it be! Amen!

(based on John 15:1-17)

Pomegranate

Unexpected Refreshment

*Saul ... was camping under a **pomegranate** tree in Migron, not far from Gibeah....*

— 1 Samuel 14:2 (TEV)

Pomegranate is mentioned in the Bible about thirty times. The above verse refers to an event shortly before Saul is rejected as king. Seemingly he spent too much time under the pomegranate tree, when he should have been depending on God and helping his son Jonathan win victories.

Pomegranate literally means "apple with grains." Inside each fruit are crowded ruby-colored seeds, each full of refreshing juice and covered with a thin skin. The pomegranate is about the size of a large apple. The tough, leathery rind is yellow overlaid with pink or rich-red. The invigorating fruit is a prized delicacy in a hot and thirsty land, such as much of Palestine.

The pomegranate is a neat, well-rounded, small tree that may reach thirty feet in height, but typically is only fifteen feet in height. The leaves are lance shaped, glossy and leathery. The tree may live as long as 200 years, but loses vigor after fifteen or twenty years. The delicate, silky scarlet flowers are almost fiery in their brilliance.

The pomegranate has many uses. The fruit can be eaten fresh or made into syrup, jelly, or wine and can be used as a flavoring. In some places druggists use the blossoms in the preparation of a medicine, an astringent, or in treating dysentery. The rind contains large amounts of tannic acid which can be used in tanning leather or in making medicine.

The pomegranate was prominent in early Bible times as indicated by its use in decorations. On the robe of the ephod, it was alternated with golden bells (Exodus 34:33-34; 39:24-26). Also, in Solomon's Temple, they were used in the decorations of two majestic bronze columns:

The top of each column was decorated with a design of interwoven chains and two rows of bronze pomegranates. The capitals were shaped like lilies, 6 feet tall ... There were 200 pomegranates in two rows around each capital.
                                    — 1 Kings 7:17-20 (TEV)

Moses mentioned pomegranates in describing the Promised Land (Deuteronomy 8:8). And when the spies returned after visiting Palestine, pomegranates were included along with figs and grapes (Numbers 13:23).

In the Song of Solomon pomegranates are mentioned in praise of the woman:

My sweetheart, my bride, is a secret garden ... there the plants flourish. They grow like an orchard of pomegranate trees and bear the finest fruits.
                                    — Song of Solomon 4:12-13 (TEV)

In Haggai 2:19, it is used as evidence of the restoration of God's favor. The pomegranate is even spoken of as the "Tree of Life" in some ancient mythology.

Lessons From The Pomegranate

At our farm home, I remember finding ripe wild plums growing and the refreshment they provide. God has used the pomegranate, which grows and produces on its own in the wild, as a reminder of his support and restoration. This fruit is also a reminder of his desire to bring unexpected refreshment when most needed. Buy a pomegranate and count the number of seeds, maybe a section at a time, then multiply. Taste the fruit and share with others.

Prayer

Spirit of the Living God, today we pray for guidance. We remember Saul's failure to follow your guidance, and he faced disappointment, defeat, and even death. We want the pomegranate to be a symbol of your generous care that brings the best delights to our lives. Guide us in the way that the Psalmist speaks of: "Take delight in the Lord, and he will give you the desires of your heart" (Psalm 37:4 RSV). O Holy Spirit be our guide today and every day.

Yes, Lord, we open our hearts to your guidance. Amen!

Lilies Of The Field

Behold The Glory

*"Consider the **lilies of the field**, how they grow; they neither toil nor spin; yet I tell you, even Solomon in all his glory was not arrayed like one of these."*
— Matthew 6:28-29 (RSV)

The word *lilies* is used only two times in the New Testament. Both of these references are to lilies of the field, a very common but beautiful flower. This *Anemone coronaria* is one of Palestine's most sensational flowers. It is so prolific, that at times it looks like a carpet of scarlet hiding the ground.

For a small plant, the blossom of the lily is not small, but a delicate, wide flower of two inches or more in diameter. With great insight, Jesus used this flower as a basis for teaching about trust and beauty. Jesus had been talking about the futility of worry and anxiety as part of his Sermon on the Mount, "Consider the birds ... consider the flowers...." A carpet of lilies of the field were surrounding Jesus as he gave this sermon.

Solomon was a king of wealth who imported the finest quality of clothing available. He dressed in lavish splendor. Jesus spoke of the beauty of the lilies, which Solomon could not contend with. The living color, delicate texture, and splendid construction of this common lily fit together to provide the basis for Jesus' teachings.

Today we may consider common lilies, violets, or dandelions as weeds. It may be annoying to see these flowers carpet our lawns or roadsides. But a single lily, violet, or dandelion can be a flower of beauty. Pick an individual blossom sometime, and look at it carefully.

Behold the glory from this verse in Matthew:

"It is God who clothes the wild grass — grass that is here today and gone tomorrow, burned up in the oven. Won't he be all the more sure to clothe you?"
— Matthew 6:30 (TEV)

29

God's care for nature is evident in the wild grass burned in Palestinian ovens. The Palestinian oven was a clay box set on bricks over the fire. When it was necessary to raise the temperature in the oven quickly, handfuls of dry grass and flowers were thrown into the oven. So the assurance is given in Matthew 6:30 that we are much more valuable in God's sight. We are chosen and loved. God's care and glory for nature is also evident.

Behold the glory of the lilies, grasses, and weeds around us. When there is so much beauty and splendor in naturally blooming flowers, why do we work so hard to cultivate flowers? I believe the splendor of the one enhances the splendor of the other. I have seen the extraordinary beauty of flowers freely growing in the Rocky Mountains, the alpine meadows, and the native prairies. Also, I have looked in wonder at formal gardens in a palatial setting and the backyard gardens of friends. No King Solomon or lavish wealth today can compare.

Lessons From Lilies Of The Field

The lilies of the field provide us with glorified information from Jesus' teachings. Using the common lily as an example, he speaks of two ways to defeat worry. First, we must realize that God cares for the lilies that may be trampled under foot. He certainly cares in a more wonderful way for us. "The very hairs of your head are all numbered" (Matthew 10:30).

Second, we must realize that worry is defeated when God, and the doing of God's will, becomes the dominating drive in our lives. In Matthew 6:34, Jesus states that worry is defeated when we live one day at a time, not worrying about tomorrow.

Prayer

Creator and Sustainer of all, in the common things like a lily, we can find extraordinary beauty. Even the delicate touch of flowers and their fragrance refresh our senses. Thank you for elegant and charming flower gardens, and for the abundant growth of wildflowers in their natural habitat. Thank you also for the common weeds and grasses we may trample under foot.

Now we consider the lilies of the field, and the call of our Lord not to worry.

With the songwriter we say:

> *Open my eyes, that I may see*
> *Glimpses of truth thou hast for me;*
> *Place in my hands the wonderful key*
> *That shall unclasp and set me free.*
> *Silently now I wait for thee,*
> *Ready my God thy will to see;*
> *Open my eyes, illumine me,*
> *Spirit divine!*
>
> — Clara H. Scott

In God's name we pray. Amen.

Lily

Rainbows Recalled

I am a rose of Sharon, a **lily** *of the valleys. As a* **lily** *among brambles ... He brought me to the banqueting house, and his banner over me was love.*

— Song of Solomon 2:1, 2, 4 (RSV)

The verses above talk about the lilies of the field that grew very prolific at the time of Jesus. The Old Testament references speak of the true lily, as we know it today.

The true family of lilies contains many horticulturally important plants. These include tulips, lilies, daffodils, hyacinths, day lilies, and amaryllis. Another family of lilies is the iris, with about 1,800 species, including crocuses, gladiolus, and lilies of the valley.

Scholars believe that the lily, referred to in the Song of Solomon, is the chalcedonicum lily. This lily has high stalks of clear green leaves mixed with bright, shiny dark green leaves. The blossoms at the top of the high stalks have the color of glowing red flame. The blossom heads bend downwards. These were highly prized lilies, and most likely made up a part of King Solomon's gardens.

Almost all lilies have an underground bulb that stores nourishment and supplies needed food for the flower, even in the drought of desert areas. Doesn't the beauty of a rainbow and the beauty of a lily remind us of God's never-ending love?

The lily can help us recall love and beauty. The Song of Solomon, in many ways, is a love letter. Flowers presented to the love of our life, whether a dozen roses or a bouquet of lilies, are treasured expressions of love and beauty. "As a lily, so is my love" (Song of Solomon 2:2 KJV).

An old Gospel hymn eloquently reminds us:

I have found a friend in Jesus — He's everything to me,
He's the fairest of ten thousand to my soul;
The Lily of the Valley — in Him alone I see
All I need to cleanse and make me fully whole.

Scott Patton

In sorrow He's my comfort, in trouble He's my stay,
He tells me every care on Him to roll;
He's the Lily of the Valley, the Bright and Morning Star,
He's the fairest of ten thousand to my soul.
— Charles W. Fry

The beauty of the Temple built by Solomon was enhanced with lilies carved in bronze:

> *Now the capitals that were on the top of the pillars in the vestibule were of lily work, four cubits high. The capitals were on the two pillars and also above the rounded projection that was beside the latticework; there were two hundred pomegranates in rows all around....* — 1 Kings 7:19-20 (NRSV)

Lessons From The Lily

Few families of flowers have as much variety of color as lilies. They remind us of the rainbow. Perhaps most fitting and symbolic is the pure white Easter lily that reminds us of the resurrection of Jesus Christ. An exciting lesson can be observed: plant some Easter lilies at home, and watch them bloom from year-to-year. Or plant an amaryllis, and watch it develop and bloom. Bring home a book about lilies from the library. See the splendor of God's creation.

Prayer

Lord Jesus, thank you for your friendship. We see a marvelous beauty in you, Lord Jesus. You are the Lily of the Valley and "the fairest of ten thousand"! May we see in you what our heart longs for and desires.

Forgive us for times when our selfish desires have pulled us away from you. Yes, Lord Jesus, as we recall a rainbow, we know your friendship and love is a promise too. Amen!

Rose (Narcissus)

The Desert Shall Rejoice

*The wilderness and the solitary place shall be glad for them; and the desert shall rejoice, and blossom as the **rose**. It shall blossom abundantly, and rejoice even with joy and singing: the glory of Lebanon shall be given unto it, the excellency of Carmel and Sharon; they shall see the glory of the Lord, and the excellency of our God.*
— Isaiah 35:1-2 (KJV)

This biblical reference to the rose in the book of Isaiah refers to the narcissus plant. Winifred Walker in *All the Plants of the Bible* writes:

In this instance the Hebrew word translated "rose" indicates a plant with a bulbous root, so it cannot apply to a true rosebush. The accepted opinion is that the little flower alluded to is the yellow Narcissus tazetta.

The rose has a dazzling golden yellow color. It grows wild throughout the area of Palestine and provides a profusion of color. The tender green shoots of this flower appear in the fall. Early in the spring, following a rain, the lovely fragrant blossoms appear.

Some flowers, like the *Narcissus tazetta*, have aromas that are very refreshing and stimulating. Today, these flowers might be used for aromatherapy. I was astonished to see a hospital bulletin board advocating the possibilities of healing help from aromas. Information was included about nurses in the United Kingdom using aromatherapy to promote relaxation and to enhance well-being. Aromas can change the body's chemistry within seconds of inhalation. This reminds me of the exhilarating aroma of apple blossoms and wild roses.

There are several types of narcissus. All of them have sword-shaped leaves and send up tall shoots. The blossom consists of six petals surrounding a trumpet-shaped tube. Daffodils are narcissus with a long trumpet as a center of the flower. Jonquils are short-trumpet

Scott Patton

narcissus. Most of the blossoms are yellow, but colors also include white and some with a crinkled red edge.

The name *narcissus* comes from the legendary Greek youth, Narcissus, who fell in love with his own reflection in a pool.

The elegance and grace of the narcissus have been celebrated in verse and story for many centuries. Homer wrote and sang of it in his "Hymn to Demeter":

> *The Narcissus wondrously glittering, a noble sight for all, whether immortal gods or mortal men; from whose root a hundred heads spring forth, and at the fragrant odour thereof all the broad heaven above, and all the earth laughed, and the salt waves of the sea.*

Regarding the rose, Isaiah may have said it better when he talked about the time of the restoration of Israel, which would be like the desert rejoicing.

Lessons From The Rose (Narcissus)

Stop and smell the roses. The aroma can be a reminder from God to stop and refresh our senses. The beauty in a narcissus blossom can turn a barren desert into rejoicing.

World-wide there are over 200,000 known varieties of flowers. Are we sharing the beauty of flowers with God and others, as he has shared it with us?

Prayer

Dear Lord, we rejoice in the coming of spring-time as displayed by the first flowers that bloom. Where least expected, flowers are blooming: from a crack in the highway, to a scorching desert, to on top of the water.

As do flowers, we want to bloom where we are planted. We can do this by serving your world-wide family and showing beauty in unexpected places. Please bless missionaries and Peace Corps workers who are providing beauty in desperate or distraught areas of the world.

Help us display beauty, like the roses, wherever hope and rejoicing is needed in God's name! We praise you, dear Lord. Amen.

Rose Of Sharon

Fairest Of The Fair

*I am a rose of Sharon, a lily of the valleys ... He brought
me to the banqueting house, and his banner over me
was love.* — Song of Solomon 2:1, 4 (RSV)

The word *rose* is used twice in the King James and Revised
Standard Versions of the Bible in Song of Solomon 2:1-2 and Isaiah
35:1. It is uncertain what plant is referred to for the word *rose*.
A. W. Anderson in his book, *Plants of the Bible*, clarifies the
use of *rose*:

> *There has been much difference of opinion about the
> true identity of the various roses mentioned in the Bible
> and almost the only point upon which the various au-
> thorities agree is that several very different plants have
> been loosely referred to under this name.*

The rose of Sharon has been identified as a bulb growing plant,
most likely the tulip, *Tulipa sharonensis*, or Sharon tulip. This specific plant is shapely and colorful. It would fit well with the theme
from the Song of Solomon.

Currently in the United States, a rose of Sharon is a large flow-
ering hibiscus shrub that may grow twelve feet high. This shrub
was not known in Bible times.

The tulip plant referred to in Bible times has glowing red flowers, is about ten inches tall, and has silver gray-green leaves. The
blossom has the shape of a turban, and in Turkey, turban is the
name which is used for this plant. The rose of Sharon grows pro-
fusely on the plain of Sharon in Palestine.

"Tiptoe Through The Tulips" became a popular love song in
the 1960s. The rose of Sharon can parallel this love song. God's
love surrounds us just like the beauty in flowers that grow wild
around us.

Scott Patton

Many writers have interpreted the rose of Sharon as a specific reference to Jesus. Truly he is "The Lily of the Valley" and "The Rose of Sharon"!

Albert A. Ketchum wrote:

He is the fairest of fair ones,
He is the Lily, the Rose.
Rivers of mercy surround Him,
Grace, love, and pity He shows.

Whether we describe Jesus like a rose, a tulip, or a lily, his banner over us is love! In times past, those with power and authority might have a large banner inscribed with their name or accomplishments. Today we can make computer-generated banners with a variety of messages. But the most glorious message a banner can display is in the opening verses from Song of Solomon, chapter 2: "... his banner over me was love." This proclaims the truth that nothing can separate us from the love of God!

Lessons From The Rose Of Sharon

God's love is like a banner over roses, tulips, and me. When we tiptoe through God's wonders, we are more aware of his presence. Take two minutes today to tiptoe! Then compile a list of words to describe Jesus (i.e.: King of kings, Rose of Sharon, etc.).

Prayer

Gracious Lord Jesus, we have seen you as the Rose of Sharon
And the Lily of the Valley.
You come to us as beauty and fragrance,
The fairest of ten thousand to my soul!
Your Love, like a banner, is unfurled over us.
Your Grace, like apple blossoms of spring time,
Embraces us and provides a lasting aroma.
Enliven us and help us to be as clay in your hands.
Melt us and mold us after your will.
May we truly be a part of the appealing aroma
That will attract others to you.
We pray in the precious name of Jesus. Amen.

Judas Tree

Forgiveness: Failed Or Forsaken?

*When **Judas**, the traitor, learned that Jesus had been
condemned, he repented and took back the thirty silver
coins to the chief priests and the elders. "I have sinned
by betraying an innocent man to death!" he said.
"What do we care about that?" they answered.
"That is your business!"*

***Judas** threw the coins down in the Temple and left;
then he went off and hanged himself.*

— Matthew 27:3-5 (TEV)

The Bible does not specify the type of tree that Judas hanged
himself from, but there is agreement among many biblical authorities that the tree was a redbud. In fact, most dictionaries and ency-
clopedias identify the tree as both a Judas tree and as a Redbud
tree. I imagine that a tree for Judas' hanging would be a twisted
and gruesome looking tree, not the colorful redbud tree.

Temperate regions of the northern hemisphere are where redbud trees grow. The tree is particularly beautiful in the spring when
the whole tree is covered with pink to red delicate blossoms. Flowers grow on both the old and new parts of its branches. The flower-
ing blossoms are sweet tasting to humans and animals. The redbud's
fruit is a flat-winged, many-seeded pod, and is a valuable source of
food for wildlife. Once the flowers blossom, the heart-shaped leaves
appear. The wood of a redbud tree is very hard and beautifully
veined. This tree can attain a height of thirty to forty feet, display-
ing its attractive blossoms, leaves, and wood.

According to legend, the pink flowers blushed rose-red with
shame when Judas chose the redbud tree to hang himself from. In
the presence of the living Christ, could Judas have found forgiveness as Peter did? Peter's denial and lying about it was a terrible
sin, when Jesus most needed companionship. Yet Peter was forgiven. Jesus can make the vilest sinner clean and forgiven, but Judas failed to hear this message and felt forsaken.

William Barclay, in his commentary on the Gospel of Mark, gives a good summary of the sin of Judas:

> *Both Luke and John say the same thing. They say quite simply, that the devil entered into Judas (Luke 22:3, John 13:27). In the last analysis that is what happened. Judas wanted Jesus to be what he wanted Him to be, and not what Jesus wanted to be. In reality Judas attached himself to Jesus, not so much to become a follower of Jesus, as to use Jesus to work out the plans and desires and schemes of his own ambitious heart. So far from surrendering to Jesus, he wanted Jesus to surrender to him, and when Jesus took His own way, the way of the Cross, Judas was so incensed that he betrayed Him. The very essence of sin is pride. The very core of sin is independence. The very heart of sin is the desire to do what we like and not what God likes. That is what the Devil, Satan, the Evil One stands for. He stands for everything which is against God and which will not bow to God. That is the very spirit which was incarnate in Judas.*
>
> *We shudder at Judas. But let us think again — covetousness, jealousy, ambition, the dominant desire to have our own way of things, Are we so very different? These are the things which made Judas betray Jesus, and these are the things which still make men betray Him in every age.*
> — *Daily Study Bible Series: The Gospel of Mark*, p. 346

Lessons From The Judas Tree

Are we like Judas who betrayed Jesus?

If the Judas tree could talk, I'm sure it would say, "I, like Judas, could have failed and felt forsaken because of being part of a terrible tragedy. Instead, I chose to become a more beautiful tree, and praise God each year with an abundance of colorful blossoms."

We can overcome the terror and tragedies that come our way through Jesus' resurrection and God's unfailing love.

Prayer

Most Gracious Lord Jesus,
We have allowed selfishness and sin to rule our lives,
Ruin our service for the needs of others,
And reverse momentum to serve you alone.
Cleanse and forgive us now,
And direct us to the road of Righteousness,
The route to renewal and revival.
All a part of transformation and regeneration,
Transform us now,
By the power and presence of Our Transformer, Jesus Christ.
In whose name we pray. Amen.

Locust Tree

Consider Coming With Confession

*At that time John the Baptist came to the desert of Judea
and started preaching. "Turn away from your sins," he
said, "because the Kingdom of heaven is near!" ...
John's clothes were made of camel's hair; he wore a
leather belt around his waist, and his food was **locusts**
and wild honey. People came to him from ... all over the
country near the Jordan River. They confessed their sins,
and he baptized them in the Jordan.*

— Matthew 3:1-2, 4-6 (TEV)

I had always assumed that the locusts referred to in the verses
above were an insect, not a tree. Scholars are certainly not in agreement, but there is evidence that the locust referred to above was the
locust tree.

In her book *All the Plants of the Bible*, Winifred Walker writes:
"The locust is the fruit of the carob tree, and accepted in the East as
the food on which Saint John the Baptist fed; thus it is known there
as Saint John's bread."

The English term for the carob tree is locust and is similar to
locust trees in the United States. The carob locust bears large pods
filled with large, edible seeds. In Luke 15:16 where the Prodigal
Son ate husks with the pigs, these were likely from the locust tree.
The seeds are very palatable to man and beast. These seeds have
been an important food for the poor in the Near East. Historians
recorded locust seeds and pods as the main source of food for
Wellington's Cavalry during the Peninsula War.

The locust tree is a medium-sized tree with dark evergreen
leaves and inconspicuous but fragrant flowers. The flowers produce narrow pods with large seeds. Good trees may yield up to
3,000 pounds of seeds and pods each year.

The rabbis tell a Rip van Winkle-style story about the locust.
Rabbi Chomi went for a walk one evening and found an old man
planting a locust seed. He asked the old man why he would do that

46

Scott Potter

because it takes thirty years for the tree to reach maturity. The old man responded that he would like to leave a tree for his children. The rabbi was weary and sat down to rest, fell asleep, and slept soundly. When he awoke the sun was rising and he hurried home lest his family worry about him. Arriving home he saw a fine locust tree standing where the old man planted the seed. Reaching the village, he found that everyone was a stranger. Gradually he became aware that he had slept for seventy years!

Lessons From The Locust Tree

God provides for you and me the way he did for John the Baptist. The locust tree is an example of God's glorious creations that he provides. Challenge yourself to eat fresh food only for at least one day. Relish in fruits, vegetables, and legumes, as John the Baptist relished eating locusts and wild honey.

Prayer

Our Creator, we need to see you as our providing Father, who helps those gone astray. Please help us return to your loving care and forgiveness. Thank you for the locust tree as a symbol of your ever-providing love. In Jesus' name. Amen!

Mulberry Tree

Seeds Of Faith And Faithful Seeds

The apostles said to the Lord, "Make our faith greater."
The Lord answered, "If you had faith as big as a mus-
tard seed, you could say to this **mulberry tree**, *'Pull*
yourself up by the roots and plant yourself in the sea!'
and it would obey you."   — Luke 16:5-6 (TEV)

The King James Version translates the tree referred to as sy-
camine instead of mulberry. Current scholars agree that the tree is
the mulberry. Although it was a common tree at the time of Jesus
in Palestine, it is only mentioned once in the Bible.

It is surprising that Bible verses include about a hundred plant
references, compared to at least 2,300 species of plants during Bible
times. Accordingly, the frequency of the mention of a particular
plant in the Bible does not indicate how common it was. Mulberry
fruit was used extensively, but only the one biblical reference is
made. In contrast, the cedar tree that is not native to Palestine, is
referred to seventy times.

A mulberry tree can attain a height of forty feet or more. Its
heart-shaped leaves are toothed. Miniature blossoms, crowded close
together, produce the blackberry-like fruit, which is prized as a
delicious and healthy treat.

Early memories of my childhood farm home include a black
mulberry tree. Good to eat raw, the mulberries were a special treat
when cooked with rhubarb. Of course the same fruit was a delight
to birds, but hazardous for our newly washed car!

The white mulberry in China provides food for silk worms.
The silk worms eat the bright green leaves, then spin a cocoon of
silk, which is harvested for silk production. This type of silk production has been tried in other nations, including the United States
and Palestine, but with little success.

Scott Patton

Lessons From The Mulberry Tree

Jesus spoke of the power of faith, even the faith of a mustard seed, which could have the power to cause a mulberry tree to transplant itself. How amazing it is that a seed can cling to life, even when neglected or trampled under foot. Seeds are faithful.

We can plant the seeds of faith. There are many people around us who are hungering and thirsting for righteousness. They are looking for examples of faith, searching for answers to spiritual questions. Pray that God will guide you to sow good seeds for his glory.

Prayer

God of the mustard seed,
Creator of the mulberry,
You call us to live by faith.

God of the sparrow,
God of the skies,
God of the weak,
God of the strong,
In faith we open our hearts
To your creative power and love.

We realize with amazement
That you have remembered the smallest and simplest,
Each benefiting from your care and concern.

May we be those who are good stewards
Of your creation, including nature and wildlife.
We pray that our concern will extend beyond nature
To include the least, the lost, the loneliest of your human
family.

Jesus we hear you reminding us,
"In as much as you have done it
Unto one of the least ...
You have done it unto me."
Amen!

Palm Tree

The Righteous Shall Flourish

*The righteous shall flourish like the **palm tree**.*
— Psalm 92:12 (KJV)

The palm tree plays a very prominent part in the plants of the Bible. Exodus 15:27 is the first place where palm tree is used. This is where Moses and the Israelites are traveling through the wilderness, and an oasis is found: "Next they came to Elim, where there were twelve springs and seventy palm trees; there they camped by the water."

Palm trees are distinct in an oasis. When traveling through a desert area, discovering a palm tree in the distance means water, a pressing necessity, is near. Thousands of Israelites were with Moses and desperate for water. At Elim they found water amid the palm trees.

Many naturalists agree that the palm is the most remarkable of all trees. One remarkable quality is its ability to withstand storms. A hurricane may blow a palm tree over, but from its prostrate position, it will again lift its head, and the growing top will become upright. Also remarkable is that the palm tree can withstand fire without being destroyed. Instead of having a layer of fragile bark like most trees, the growth is from within. A complete outer layer of bark could be removed, and the tree would not be destroyed. The palm tree's height is a remarkable feature, with some trees reaching 100 feet in height.

Virtually all human needs can be met in the amazing palm tree. The date palm, referred to in the Bible, can provide food, shelter, and clothing. This tree provides more agricultural wealth and nutritional food per acre than perhaps any other tree. Palm branches can be used as a building material, and palm leaves can be used for clothing. Also, they are satisfactory for use as fuel for a fire. The Palmyra palm tree of India has about 800 different uses. Worldwide there are more than 1,500 different kinds of palms. In Bible usage, the palm tree is referred to 32 times.

Another unusual quality of the palm tree is its growth point, known as the terminal bud. It is at the very top of the tree, from which growth takes place. If the terminal bud is not disturbed, almost nothing can destroy the tree. Fire can burn around it, a storm can blow it over, and it will continue to flourish. But if the bud is destroyed, the tree dies. Regrettably, the terminal bud is considered a delicacy called palm cabbage. In some nations, it is harvested to eat, thus destroying the tree.

Palm Sunday is a significant day in the Christian year. In celebration of Jesus entering Jerusalem, palm branches were cut from nearby palm trees and waved in his honor or placed on the ground before him. Palm branches were an accepted tribute for royalty.

Lessons From The Palm Tree

> *The righteous will flourish like palm trees; they will grow like the cedars of Lebanon. They are like trees planted in the house of the Lord, that flourish in the Temple of our God, that still bear fruit in old age and are always green and strong.*
> — Psalm 92:12-14 (TEV)

We could have the terminal bud symbolize our living relationship with God. Keep that relationship active and growing. Even if the storms and fires come, we will endure. If we destroy our relationship with God, all that is valuable in life is destroyed.

Prayer

Gracious God, thank you for palm trees providing coconuts, dates, and much more. May we, as righteous people, flourish like the palm. Help us meet the storms or fires of life, and never be defeated. Thank you for the victory you give us in Jesus Christ our Lord. Amen!

Sycamore Tree

Is Climbing Learning?

Jesus went on into Jericho and was passing through.
There was a chief tax collector there named Zacchaeus,
who was rich. He was trying to see who Jesus was, but
he was a little man and could not see Jesus because of
the crowd. So he ran ahead of the crowd and climbed a
sycamore tree *to see Jesus.* — Luke 19:1-4 (TEV)

The sycamore tree of the Bible is not the same as the sycamore in the United States. The spelling is the same, although the King James Version uses the "sycomore" spelling. The tree of the Bible is a curious-looking tree that combines the characteristics of both the fig and mulberry, and is often called a "mulberry fig." The fruit grows directly from the trunk on little sprigs in clusters, like the grape. To make the fruit more edible, a few days before gathering, the fruit would be punctured with a sharp instrument or specially shaped fingernail. The sycamore tree grows to the size of a walnut tree, and its wide spreading branches provide plentiful shade.

The sycamore has a large trunk with fairly low branches, thus being ideal for Zacchaeus to climb. If he had never climbed the tree, the meeting with Jesus and the marvelous learning experience that took place later in Zacchaeus' home would never have taken place.

The tree was extensively used and of great importance in Palestine and Egypt. The wood is porous but very enduring, making its chief use for lumber. The lumber was used for furniture and buildings or for fashioning mummy chests, which have been found in perfect condition after 3,000 years.

King David's appointment of an overseer for sycamore trees in 1 Chronicles 27:28 proves that the sycamore tree was very important in Bible times. 1 Kings 10:27 speaks of the abundance of this tree, "plentiful as the sycamore of the Shephelah." Because of its prevalent growth along trails and roadsides, poor families often depended on the sycamore to provide food and fuel.

55

The prophet Amos gives a significant witness to God's call:

> *Then Amos answered Amaziah, "I am no prophet, nor a prophet's son; but I am a herdsman, and a dresser of sycamore trees, and the Lord took me from following the flock, and the Lord said to me, 'Go, prophesy to my people Israel.' "* — Amos 7:14-15 (RSV)

Lessons From The Sycamore Tree

Many stories were told under sycamore trees, since they were so abundant and provided refreshing shade. In addition to calling Zacchaeus from the tree, Jesus undoubtedly sat under sycamores with his disciples and told them some of the marvelous stories in the New Testament, perhaps teaching about the Prodigal Son or the Good Samaritan. Imagine yourself sitting at the feet of Jesus under the shade of the spreading sycamore tree.

Prayer

Heavenly Father, we remember how Zacchaeus had a hunger in his heart that only you could satisfy. He found a way to climb above the obstacles around him and meet you, Lord Jesus. And seeing in you the Way, the Truth, and the Life, he came down from the sycamore tree. Zacchaeus' life was transformed.

We pray that you would strengthen us to climb the trees, the ladders, or the mountains that may block our way, as we seek to follow where you lead.

In the strength of Jesus we pray. Amen!

Willow Tree

Hang Your Harp

*By the rivers of Babylon we sat down; there we wept when we remembered Zion. On the **willows** near by we hung up our harps. Those who captured us told us to sing ... How can we sing a song to the Lord in a foreign land? May I never be able to play the harp again if I forget you....* — Psalm 137:1-5 (TEV)

Some scholars have suggested that the willow, referred to above, was the weeping willow tree. Other scholars interpret it to be the poplar tree. There is no way to tell for certain, but weeping willows do grow along the streams where the Israelites were exiled in Babylon. How fittingly symbolic the weeping willow would be, because of the tears the Israelites shed in captivity. The songs, no doubt, helped keep their faith alive, and their captors must have found the music helpful and enjoyable. But when requested to "perform" for their captors, the Israelites refused.

Globally, there are about 300 species of willows. They range in size from a tiny shrub only inches high to trees more than 120 feet high. The wood is very bendable, and is used to make baskets and furniture. The bitter bark yields tannin, which is used to tan leather. Also, salicene can be extracted, which is used by scientists in biochemical tests and as a substitute for quinine.

The beautiful willow leaves are long and narrow, tapering to a point, with finely toothed edges. The upper surface of the leaf is clear rich-green, and the underside is usually white or silver colored.

Early in the spring most willows produce upright clusters of tiny, yellowish-green flowers known as catkins. Catkins literally comes from "cat" because some of the clusters resemble a cat's tail. As it develops, the female flower produces a flask-shaped pod that splits open when mature, releasing tiny seeds with white, silky hairs.

In Palestine, willows grow abundantly along the streams, where they multiply very rapidly. They are valuable next to a stream to help hold the river bank in place. The roots interlace, forming a

Scott Patton

tough network that holds the soil together and prevents erosion. Willows are also helpful in marshy areas, where there may be too much water, because the roots suck up large amounts of water.

The passage below refers to willows along the streams.

> *I will give water to the thirsty land and make streams flow on the dry ground. I will pour out my power on your children and my blessing on your descendants. They will thrive like well-watered grass, like willows by streams of running water.* — Isaiah 44:3-4 (TEV)

Willow branches have been used by the Jews in some of their religious ceremonies. The branches were used for building the tent for the feast of Booths (Leviticus 23:40).

Lessons From The Willow Tree

The willow does not supply food, but it is a versatile tree, providing a variety of useful items, including furniture, medicine, fuel, tannin, and shelter. On the farm, I learned how to make fine whistles from willow. The bark slips off easily, and with a little cutting with a pocket knife, the whistle is complete. An unusual use was the making of a high grade of charcoal from the wood; charcoal was once used to make gunpowder.

Prayer

Gracious God, while we may never have experienced actual captivity, or living as refugees in a foreign land, we have faced times of depression, estrangement, rejection, and separation from loved ones. Even in dark hours you have been with us. You have lifted us with your love and put a song in our heart because of Jesus. Even when the storms are raging, you stand by us and give us a song of assurance.

We remember in our prayer those who are refugees, some even slaves, those who have been torn away from their homeland, who like the children of Israel cannot sing a song of the Lord on foreign soil. Thank you for the arm of the church that reaches those most in need. Use our arms, our hands, and our gifts to reach them also.

In the strong name of Jesus we pray. Amen.

Cedar

Build A Stately Mansion

*... like a **cedar** in Lebanon, with beautiful, shady
branches, a tree so tall it reaches the clouds ... Because
it was well-watered, it grew taller than other trees. Its
branches grew thick and long.*

— Ezekiel 31:3, 5 (TEV)

More than one type of cedar tree is mentioned in the Bible.
Cedar is mentioned as being a part of the preparation for sacrifice
in Leviticus 14. Also it is referred to in Numbers 24:6. Most prominent and magnificent is the cedar of Lebanon. The fragrance and
the quality of the wood is so superior that it was chosen as the
building material for the Temple.

*Solomon sent to Huram [Hiram] the king of Tyre, say-
ing, "As thou didst deal with David my father, and didst
send him cedars to build him a house to dwell in, even
so deal with me ... Send me also cedar trees, fir trees,
and algum trees out of Lebanon ... and, behold, my servants shall be with thy servants, even to prepare me
timber in abundance: for the house which I am about
to build shall be wonderful great...."*

— 2 Chronicles 2:3, 8-9 (KJV)

*So King Hiram supplied Solomon with all the cedar
and pine logs that he wanted ... The inside walls were
covered with cedar panels from the floor to the ceiling,
and the floor was made of pine ... It was thirty feet long
and was partitioned off by cedar boards reaching from
the floor to the ceiling ... The cedar panels were decorated with carvings of gourds and flowers; the whole
interior was covered with cedar....*

— 1 Kings 5:10; 6:15, 16, 18 (TEV)

It would be a marvelous experience to enter the Temple with the rich fragrance of cedar surrounding you. There are other places in the Bible where the cedar tree is extolled. See Psalm 92:12, Song of Solomon 1:17, 5:15, and 8:9, and Isaiah 14:8.

With its multitude of uses, the cedar's fame was known through the civilized world of the Near East. At one time these trees were plentiful in Lebanon and parts of Palestine. Some soar over 120 feet in the air with durable, useful trunks six to eight feet in diameter. During Bible times, the cedar tree was prized for building homes, palaces, furniture, and instruments. With its resistance to water, it was ideal for ship building and ship masts.

Today there are only a few prized cedars of Lebanon left. Often they were unwisely used, not replanted, devastated by war, or used as fuel for fires. Just as redwood trees are protected in the United States, the few remaining cedars in Palestine and Lebanon are diligently protected. The distinctive pyramid image of the cedar of Lebanon adorns the modern flag of that country.

This tree bears a cone that takes three years to mature. During the first year it is small and pale green. The second year, the cone reaches its full size, about three inches long. The third year, the tiny seeds, now a deep brown color, are scattered from the cone, and the cone falls.

Fortunately, the cedar tree lives on. The heritage has been passed into a genetic pool of new generations. Some are grown in England, France, and the United States. A few specialized nurseries make cedar seeds and plants available.

Lessons From The Cedar

Oliver Wendell Holmes, in his poem "The Chambered Nautilus," challenges us to live similar to the nautilus:

> *Build thee more stately mansions, O my soul,*
> *As the swift seasons roll!*
> *Leave thy low-vaulted past!*
> *Let each new temple, nobler than the last,*
> *Shut thee from heaven with a dome more vast,*
> *Till thou at length art free,*
> *Leaving thine out-grown shell by life's unresting sea!*

I see the cedar as a call to build a life given in service for God, even as the temple was built from the cedar wood.

Prayer

O Thou Great Builder of the souls of men, women, and children, guide me today with your purpose. The cedar wood has been used to build man-made objects to glorify you. Please be with our children in the process of building their lives. Help each of us build a spiritual temple fit for you to live in at the heart of our lives. Amen!

Ebony

The Patriarch Of Woods

*The people of Rhodes traded with you; people of many coastal lands gave you ivory and **ebony** in exchange for your goods.*　　　　— Ezekiel 27:15 (TEV)

Ebony is mentioned only once in the Bible. It is not grown in Palestine, but as the passage from Ezekiel points out, it was a valuable commodity brought in through buying or bartering.

Ebony comes from the tree that goes by the same name. It comes from a large tree that grows in Africa, South America, and some countries of the Far East including India, Japan, and the Philippines.

Only the dark, usually black, inner wood is usable. The outer wood is rather white and is of little value. A good trunk can be large enough to yield a heartwood log of two feet in diameter and fifteen feet long. The tree has large stout leaves and small bell-shaped cream-colored flowers.

It might be called the patriarch of woods because it is strong, durable, and ages well. Carvings of ebony wood that are centuries old still are beautiful and durable. Some of the world's finest furniture has been made from ebony, and ebony has been used for inlays on the finest furniture. For years ebony was considered the best material for black piano keys.

Ebony is a favorite of wood carvers. Though very hard, it has a wonderful texture for woodcarving. And to the woodcarver's delight, it will take and hold a glistening polish. Since ebony is resistant to decay or water damage, it may well last many centuries even if it is not given ideal care.

I am reminded of the words of Jeremiah. He was in the potter's house talking about reworking an imperfect container so that it would be usable. God said to Jeremiah, "... Don't I have the right to do with you ... what the potter did with the clay?" (Jeremiah 18:6 TEV).

Unlike clay, ebony is not pliable, but it is workable. This is the way we should be in the hands of the Master workman.

The word *ebony* comes from the Hebrew word *eben*, meaning a stone. And the name *Ebenezer* literally means "stone of help." Ebony was so prized in some cultures that, along with gold, it was the only suitable tribute accepted by kings.

Lessons From Ebony

Black is beautiful. Sometimes blackness is associated with night, darkness, and trouble. But a wonderful truth is that whether it's skin, clothing, or ebony wood, black is beautiful.

With the truths we have noted about ebony, we could say or sing:

Have thine own way Lord; have thine own way.
You are the carver; I am your ebony.
Shape me and pare me after thy will.
I will be waiting, yielded and still.

Prayer

O Divine Creator, out of soil, sunshine, and the miracle of growth, you have turned mud and light into material we call ebony. Bless the efforts of those who work to preserve forests here and rainforests elsewhere. Bless the efforts of those who plant trees to provide for the generations yet unborn. Thank you for the rich heritage of a vast variety of trees throughout the world. We dedicate ourselves to be good stewards and conservationists to your glory. Amen!

Oak

A Place Of Burial Or Resurrection?

*Jacob came with all his people to Luz, which is now known as Bethel, in the land of Canaan. He built an altar there and named the place for the God of Bethel, because God had revealed himself to him there when he was running away from his brother. Rebecca's nurse Deborah died and was buried beneath the **oak** south of Bethel. So it was named "**Oak** of Weeping."*

— Genesis 35:6-8 (TEV)

The Bible refers to more than one burial under an oak tree (Genesis 35 and 1 Chronicles 10:12). There was a permanence about the oak tree that made it a fitting landmark and place of burial. Even more significant is that the oak was a reminder of renewal or resurrection. Isaiah 6 talks about the coming time of destruction or exile, then includes:

Yet a tenth — a remnant — will survive; and though Israel is invaded again and again and destroyed, yet Israel will be like an oak cut down, whose stump still lives to grow again. — Isaiah 6:13 (TLB)

The oak stump is a reminder of the hoped-for revival of the nation.

Judges 9:6 is another significant passage about an oak: "Then all the men of Shechem and Bethmillo got together and went to the sacred oak tree at Shechem, where they made Abimelech king" (TEV). So the crowning of a king under an oak tree was considered significant!

The 275 species of oak trees grow nearly world-wide. Palestine has at least six species. Most common in Palestine are the holly or holm oak and the Valonia oak. In every nation, the oak has stood for strength and long life. Some types of oaks may live as long as 1,000 years, and with care, things made of oak can last

over 1,000 years. Oak is durable and resistant to rot. Most ships were made of oak until metal came into use. The acorns which all oaks produce as seeds are useful. Wild turkeys and pigs find them a choice part of their diet. Properly prepared acorns from certain types of oaks are edible. Some Native Americans ground them into meal for use.

The holly oak, one of the more common in Palestine, is a magnificent tree. The tree may become eighty feet in height. The large leaves resemble enlarged holly leaves with the edges bristling with spines. The holly oak's top has a shiny green surface and a yellow underside. The seed, or acorn, is less than an inch in length, held in a yellow-green cup.

The roots of an oak tree reach a great depth, so the tree does well in dry and very dry soil, but does not do well in swampy soil. The oak produces a very durable and beautiful wood. Some of the finest furniture available is oak. Also floors and the best house trimming material are made of oak. Where wood is burned, oak is the best fuel available.

Lessons From The Oak

Hoole, a poet from the past, includes some helpful lessons:

> *A sturdy oak, which nature forms*
> *To brave a hundred winter's storms,*
> *While round its head the whirlwinds blow,*
> *Remains with root infix'd below.*
> *When fell'd to earth, a ship it sails*
> *Through dashing waves and driving gales*
> *And now at sea, again defies*
> *The threat'ning clouds and howling skies.*

Yes, the mighty oak represents strength, bravery, beauty, and durability. Qualities offered to us by God.

Prayer

O Lord, truly we want to be like a tree,
Planted by the Living Waters of Life,
Whose source is your presence, O God.

Thank you for the oak tree that represents
Durability, strength for life, and
Strength to face the storms, even death.
Be with those now who are facing storms of
Disappointment, fear, depression, or pain,
Heal them with your love and grace.
Instill within them the oak-like qualities we see in Jesus.
In whose name we pray.
Yes, and Amen!

Pine

To Beautify The Sanctuary Of The Lord

*The wood of the **pine**, the juniper, and the cypress, the finest wood from the forests of Lebanon, will be brought to rebuild you, Jerusalem, to make my Temple beautiful, to make my city glorious.* — Isaiah 60:13 (TEV)

The writers of the Bible had unclear knowledge about the varieties of "needle evergreens." We commonly lump them all together as "evergreen." The common biblical term is "pine," and interestingly the true scientific inclusive term today is "pine," which includes, firs, cedars, spruces, hemlocks, and a variety of other evergreens.

Along with the cedars of Lebanon, pine trees were brought from Lebanon by Solomon for the building of the Temple. 1 Kings 5 and 6 tell of the massive project of bringing the wood and building the temple. Hiram was the king of Tyre who had control of the Lebanon forests.

Then Hiram sent Solomon the following message: "I have received your message, and I am ready to do what you ask. I will provide the cedars and the pine trees. My men will bring the logs down from Lebanon to the sea and will tie them together in rafts to float them down the coast to the place you choose." ... So Hiram supplied Solomon with all the cedar and pine logs that he wanted.... — 1 Kings 5:8-10 (TEV)

Soon the Temple became an exquisitely beautiful place filled with the aroma of cedar. The pine would have added the splendid radiance that only fine wood can give. As indicated, pine was an inclusive term, and this chosen "pine" from Lebanon likely was the Cilician fir. This fir is an elegant tree whose finished wood would have qualified to adorn the majestic temple.

73

The cone of this pine, when cut lengthwise, has a mark resembling a hand. One legend suggests this represents the hand of Christ and is a mark of his blessing.

A similar fir, the Nordmann or Caucasian fir, can grow to a majestic 150 feet. The needles are shiny dark-green with white lines beneath; when bruised the foliage gives off the scent of orange peel. The smooth bark of the tree is gray-brown, and the large six-inch cones are first green then turn red brown. They are favorites for decorations.

Lessons From The Pine

A tree must give up its life in order for its inner beauty to be revealed. Further elegance is evident as the wood is submitted to planing and sanding, which is harsh but necessary treatment. Sometimes we must face pain in order for hidden strengths to become evident.

Prayer

God, who touchest earth with beauty,
Make my heart anew;
With thy spirit recreate me,
Pure and strong and true.
Like the straightness of the pine trees
Let me upright be.
Like thy dancing waves in sunlight
Make me glad and free.
Like the arching of the heavens
Lift my thoughts above;
Turn my dreams to noble action,
Ministries of love.
— Mary S. Edgar

Bitter Herbs

Keeping The Passover

*And the Lord spake unto Moses, saying, Speak unto the children of Israel, saying ... he shall keep the passover unto the Lord. The fourteenth day of the second month at even they shall keep it, and eat it with unleavened bread and **bitter herbs**. They shall leave none of it unto the morning, nor break any bone of it: according to all the ordinances of the passover they shall keep it.*
— Numbers 9:9-10, 11-12 (KJV)

The Passover is a most holy festival for the Jewish people and nation. It might be compared to our Independence Day, the Fourth of July. It celebrates their deliverance from being slaves in Egypt, and the fact that they were set free. In Exodus 11 the warning of the death of the firstborn is given. Chapter 12 tells how the Children of Israel could avoid the death of their firstborn. A one-year-old lamb would be slain, and some of the blood would be put on the doorpost above the door. The angel of death, seeing that blood, would pass over the household, and their family would be spared. Death came to those with no blood over the doorpost. The Passover has been celebrated ever since, as a reminder of how God delivered them.

Preparation for the Passover included eating unleavened bread and bitter herbs. This was to remind the people that they had to leave in haste; there was no time to wait for yeast to rise for the bread. And bitter herbs were included to remind them of the bitterness of their slavery in Egypt.

Several plants have been used as bitter herbs, including endive, chicory, lettuce, sorrel, and even dandelion. The early leaves of dandelions have a good flavor and can be eaten like lettuce. Later in the growing season, the leaves are still edible, but become bitter. Dandelion and chicory roots can be ground and used as decoctions or may be added to coffee as adulterants.

75

Early colonists brought this bitter herb, the dandelion, from Europe to America as a source of greens. Since then it has spread all through the nation and is considered a pesky weed. Its name comes from the French *dent de lion*, meaning lion's tooth. The leaves are long and narrow, with sharp edges pointing down reminding one of lion's teeth.

The golden yellow head of the dandelion blossom is really a cluster of tiny flowers. It has a smooth, straight, and hollow stem. Many children have made necklaces with the stems of these bitter herbs.

Lessons From Bitter Herbs

Is it a worthless weed or a valuable plant? It can be a source of food, and in some places the white juice or latex that comes from the entire plant has been used. Maybe we should occasionally eat a bitter herb to remind us of how bitter life is without the joy, freedom, and new life in Jesus.

Prayer

Dear Heavenly Father, may we have eyes to see in the pesky dandelion a gift that can be used to benefit humanity. Thank you for the biblical account of the Passover. Lord Jesus, you are the Lamb that takes away the sins of the world. We need not fear death, because your life was given that we might have the gift of eternal life. In your name we pray. Amen!

Cinnamon

An Oil Of Holy Ointment

*The Lord said to Moses, "Take the finest spices — 12 pounds of liquid myrrh, 6 pounds of sweet-smelling **cinnamon**, 6 pounds of sweet-smelling cane, and 12 pounds of cassia. Add one gallon of olive oil, and make a sacred anointing oil, mixed like perfume.*
— Exodus 30:22-25 (TEV)

Cinnamon belongs to the laurel family and consists of about 250 species of evergreen trees, native to Ceylon from which its name comes. Highly aromatic compounds are present primarily in the bark, but also in the leaves, twigs, and berries. The leaves are strongly veined, and the flowers are small and pale-yellow in delicate sprays. Small fleshy berries develop containing a single seed. Cinnamon has always been highly prized as a spice and fragrance.

For centuries the source of cinnamon was kept a secret by the Arabs who sold it to the world's markets at an inflated price. Cinnamon is now readily available worldwide at a reasonable price.

The plants grow as high as thirty feet, but for harvesting are usually dwarfed by cutting the tree close to the lower buds. The branches are peeled for use as cinnamon. As the bark dries, it curls up and turns light brown. The long little curls are ideal for packaging and selling the cinnamon. Cinnamon oil is prepared from the leaves, fruit, and root of the plant. The fragrant oil has many uses.

The word *cinnamon* is used only four times in the Bible. *Ointment* is used 33 times, with nineteen of these times in the Old Testament. Most of the Old Testament uses would be the ointment that contained cinnamon. In Revelation 18:13, the precious possessions of Babylon are spoken of where cinnamon is included: "... cinnamon, and odors, and ointments, and frankincense...."

Most ointments contained a base of olive oil, to which aromatic spices were added. The ointments were used for anointing, medicine, beautification, fragrance, and embalming in Egypt. A

great many small, delicate flasks have been found by archaeologists that would have been used to hold ointments.

Ointments were a precious part of both the secular and sacred lives of the people of the Bible. Anointing the head with oil as a form of hospitality is mentioned in Psalm 23:35, 92:10, and 133:2. Ointments also symbolized a sacred consecration. Kings were anointed. See 1 Samuel 10:1, 1 Kings 1:39, and 2 Kings 9:1. The introductory verses refer to the ointment of the tabernacle. The healing properties of ointments are well attested in Isaiah 1:6, in Jeremiah 8:22, and in Luke 10:34, which says of the Good Samaritan: "He went to him and bound up his wounds, pouring on oil and wine; then he set him on his own beast and brought him to an inn, and took care of him" (Luke 10:34 RSV).

Lessons From Cinnamon

Many ordinary things became holy when they were anointed with the cinnamon enriched ointment. Unexpectedly Saul and then David were transformed into holy channels for God's use after being anointed. Both failed in some ways, but anointing meant a change of heart and purpose. See 1 Samuel 10 and 1 Samuel 16:13, which states: "Samuel took the oil and anointed David in front of his brothers. Immediately the Spirit of the Lord took control of David and was with him from that day on" (TEV).

Whether literally or spiritually, God's call is a call to holiness, meaning to be whole physically, mentally, and spiritually.

Prayer

Holy Lord, may we understand that your call to holiness is not a call to radical spirituality, but a call to serve you. In Jesus we see holiness perfected. We see your purpose in Jesus' life: sharing a wedding, rejoicing in transformed lives, healing the broken, and washing the feet of his disciples.

Anoint us with the indwelling presence of your Holy Spirit. And may we thus be set apart to do your holy will. We need your strength, your guidance, and your purpose. May we truly be born anew, born again, born from above, as we seek to serve you each day. Amen!

Desire

What Do You Desire?

*Remember your creator in the days of your youth, be-
fore the days of trouble come ... when one is afraid ...
the grasshopper drags itself along, and **desire** fails;
because all must go to their eternal home....*
— Ecclesiastes 12:1, 5 (NRSV)

Some translators have used the English "desire fails" as a part of the trouble that comes in old age, which the writer is talking about in Ecclesiastes 12. The Hebrew dictionary clarifies that this is a plant: "abiyownah ... the caper berry." Thus the original Hebrew reads: "the caper berry shall fail."

The desire or caper ranges in growth in the wild from Mediterranean shores to southern Asia, Australia, and the Pacific region. Where the roundish, leathery leaves join the main stem, there are two curved spiny thorns. The fluffy cream flowers, two or three inches across, appear in May in Palestine. At the center of the flower grows a cluster of rose-magenta filaments with golden-yellow tips. And in the middle is one long green pistil.

For human consumption, the flower buds are harvested before they show any color. Then they are pickled in a brew of wine vinegar and salt. They are used as seasoning, especially in a tasty meat sauce. Though it may look attractive, the two and one half inch long berry is not edible.

There is another interpretation possibility for Ecclesiastes 12:5. As the infirmities of old age come, the tasty enjoyment once experienced using the desire sauce is gone. Taste and appetite can be among the first to leave an aging person. The stimulation from the seasoning with desire is diminished.

Only once in the Bible, is the word *desire* used in reference to this caper plant. In the other 225 references, it is used as we would normally use the term today.

Scott Patton

Lessons From The Desire

Just as the "desire" caper plant can be used for a good seasoning or misused by trying to eat the dangerous berry, our desires can be used or misused.

Galatians 5:16-17 gives a helpful warning:

> *Live by the Spirit, I say, and do not gratify the desires of the flesh. For what the flesh desires is opposed to the Spirit, and what the Spirit desires is opposed to the flesh....* (NRSV)

And James 1:14-15 warns:

> *A person is tempted when he is drawn away and trapped by his own evil desires. Then his evil desire conceives and gives birth to sin; and sin, when it is full-grown, gives birth to death.* (TEV)

In contrast, notice Psalm 37:3-5:

> *Trust in the Lord and do good; live in the land and be safe. Seek your happiness in the Lord, and he will give you your heart's desire. Give yourself to the Lord; trust in him, and he will help you....* (TEV)

Prayer

Lord Jesus, I confess that often my desires have separated me from the good things you have in store for me. I have allowed evil desire to draw me away from your holy will. Just now guide me to find my heart's desire, because I have sought my happiness with the Lord. Amen!

Here and now I give myself to you. I ask your Holy Spirit to be my guide. Yes, this is the commitment I make to you in Jesus' name! Amen!

Dill

A Teacher, A Preacher, A Hypocrite?

*"Woe to you, scribes and Pharisees, hypocrites! For you tithe mint, **dill**, and cummin, and have neglected the weightier matters of the law: justice and mercy and faith. It is these you ought to have practiced, without neglecting the others. You blind guides! You strain out a gnat but swallow a camel!"*
— Matthew 23:23-24 (NRSV)

According to the dictionary, a hypocrite is one who plays a part, someone who is a "pretender." Pretending can be fun, but when someone says, "I love and follow God," while in reality they love only themselves and follow their own self-interest, that person is pretending to be what they are not and is a hypocrite. Regrettably teachers, preachers, and others who have leadership roles are most subject to being pretenders.

Dill, translated "anise" in the King James Version, is a useful plant that grows wild in Palestine and in many other places in the world. It grows three feet high and has fine-cut leaves of clear green. It has flowers of bright yellow that form an umbel (umbrella-like flower clusters). It produces an oval fruit that is brown and hard with a pungent taste. From ancient times, foods have been flavored with the plant. The flowers, leaves, and seeds all have been used to give a strong, aromatic taste to food. Dill pickles take their name from the dill written about here. Dill has been used medicinally and to promote healing for skin wounds. Currently in India, some areas use it as a universal natural medication. In some places it is used to soothe ailments ranging from hiccups to insomnia, and at one time it was used to guard against witchcraft.

The Bible mentions the importance of tithing and how it should be done with dill. The importance of the tithe is referred to in Deuteronomy 14:22, Leviticus 27:30, and other places in the Bible.

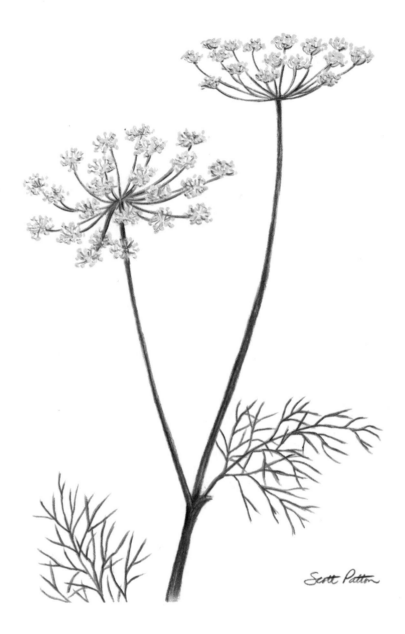

Scott Patton

William Barclay clarifies the meaning of "tithe" mentioned in Matthew 23:23 in his *Daily Study Bible Series*:

> *This tithe was holy specially for the support of the Levites, whose task it was to do the material work of the Temple. The things which had to be tithed were further defined by the Law — "everything which is eatable, and is preserved, and has its nourishment from the soil, is liable to be tithed." It is laid down: "Of dill one must tithe the seeds, the leaves and the stalks."*
>
> *The mint and dill and cummin are herbs of the kitchen garden, and would not be grown in any quantity ... To tithe them would be to tithe an infinitesimally small crop.*
>
> *... Only those who were superlatively meticulous would tithe the single plants of the kitchen garden. That is precisely what the Pharisees were like ... Yet these same men might be guilty of injustice; they were hard and arrogant and cruel, and forgot the claims of mercy ... In other words, they kept the trifles of the law, and forgot the things which really matter. That spirit is not dead; it never will be dead until Christ rules in the hearts of everyone ... There is nothing easier than to observe all the outward actions of religion and yet to be completely irreligious.*
>
> *— The Gospel of Matthew*, pp. 324-325

Lessons From The Dill

We want the dill to remind us of tithing. The Bible guides us towards giving to God's work a tithe of ten percent. Most basic is the importance of giving proportionately. The glory of God will receive what we can give. God has blessed true stewardship beyond measure.

> *Give to others, and God will give to you. Indeed, you will receive a full measure, a generous helping, poured into your hands — all that you can hold. The measure you use for others is the one that God will use for you.*
> *— Luke 6:38 (TEV)*

Prayer

Loving Lord, forgive us for those times we have been pretenders. It has been for our own benefit or to satisfy our personal ambition, when we pretend to be generous in our service and giving to you.

Thank you for the truly generous and righteous people in the past whose giving has made possible the Church today, which includes beautiful buildings, marvelous colleges, seminaries, and campsites. May our giving of time, service, and material gifts make possible the continuing growth of the spiritual dimensions of the Church by the guidance and power of your Holy Spirit. We pray in Jesus' name. Amen!

Frankincense

For Holiness

When they saw the star, they rejoiced with exceeding great joy. And when they were come into the house, they saw the young child with Mary his mother, and fell down and worshiped him; and when they had opened their treasures, they presented unto him gifts; gold, and **frankincense,** *and myrrh.*
— Matthew 2:10-11 (KJV)

Frankincense is referred to 21 times in the Bible. The word literally means "pure incense," and was a part of the most holy preparations for sacrifice, as God directed.

The Lord said to Moses: Mix equal amounts of the costly spices stacte, onycha, galbanum, and pure frankincense, then add salt to make the mixture pure and holy. Pound some of it into powder and sprinkle it in front of the sacred chest, where I meet with you. Be sure to treat this incense as something very holy. It is truly holy because it is dedicated to me, so don't ever make any for yourselves. If you ever make any of it to use as perfume, you will no longer belong to my people.
— Exodus 30:22, 34-38 (CEV)

No other incense was permitted on the altar. Incense compounded according to any other recipe could neither be offered to God nor even displayed in the holy place.

Frankincense was very expensive, partly because it was not grown in Palestine, but had to be imported from Ethiopia, Somaliland, or India. Often it came by camel caravan from Sheba, as mentioned in Isaiah 60:6 and Jeremiah 6:20. The frankincense tree, from which the resin comes, is a majestic tree with clear green leaves, comparable to the mountain ash. The wood is heavy and durable, and has a variety of uses. It has lovely star-shaped pink

flowers with lemon-colored centers. To obtain the resin, near the end of February some of the bark is cut, and a thin layer is pealed off. A month later the process is repeated, and then the resin flows out from the inner wood. When it has hardened, it is recognized as the finest burning resin, or incense, in the world.

The wise men presented gold, frankincense, and myrrh to Jesus. Gold was a reminder of his kingship, frankincense symbolized holiness, and myrrh symbolized the suffering our Lord would endure.

Lessons From Frankincense

Frankincense can represent our desire to be holy before the Lord. We can be a part of a sweet aroma that gives praise to God and attracts others to follow him.

Prayer

With thanksgiving we remember, Gracious Lord,
That one of the gifts brought to Jesus was frankincense;
A reminder of holiness,
A reminder of a pure life,
A reminder that we are all called
To a life of purity and holiness.
Your call is not to holiness that
Isolates us from being in touch with the world
Or the needs of others.
Your purity is a call to Christ-centered caring,
A call to lifting and loving.
Lord, make me more holy.
In the strong name of Jesus, we pray. Amen!

Garlic

For The Soul

*There were foreigners traveling with the Israelites. They had a strong craving for meat, and even the Israelites themselves began to complain: "If only we could have some meat! In Egypt we used to eat all the fish we wanted, and it cost us nothing. Remember the cucumbers, the watermelons, the leeks, the onions, and the **garlic** we had? But now our strength is gone. There is nothing at all to eat — nothing but this manna day after day!"* — Numbers 11:4-6 (TEV)

In the book *How the Grinch Stole Christmas*, by Dr. Seuss, these lines appear:

You're a monster, Mr. Grinch,
Your heart's an empty hole,
Your brain is full of spiders,
You've got garlic in your soul.

We know what he means in terms of garlic being associated with bad breath or strange eating habits. On the other hand, new research shows that garlic is one of the best health promoters we can eat. The Israelites remembered enjoying garlic in Egypt, where those ancient wise folks knew some things about garlic that we are just re-discovering. Garlic was even worshiped in Egypt, and the Greek Olympians consumed it to help their performance. Most of the best chefs today use garlic as an ingredient in fine cooking.

It was suitable to remember garlic as a good-tasting flavor, but when the Israelites complained to God about their food supply, they were forgetting the goodness of God in supplying manna and their safe travel. God knew their needs long before they asked. I am confident that meat, in the form of quail, would have been supplied just as soon. Their complaining only got them into trouble.

Scott Patton

92

Garlic was one of the staple foods in Egypt, where it grew in abundance. The bulb, somewhat like an onion in appearance, is composed of smaller bulblets known as cloves. The cloves can be easily separated, and each one used to provide flavoring for a dish of food. Some believe that eating the raw cloves can help the body resist colds and help with a variety of other problems.

When it blooms, a large cluster of flowers, white with tints of purple, make up a globe-like blossom. The green leaves are long and ribbon-like.

One of the Egyptian pyramids has inscriptions indicating that the 100,000 workers toiled for thirty years in construction and ate garlic, leeks, and onions to the value of 1,600 talents of silver (about $4 million).

For years garlic has held secrets of restoring health that are now being proved. A recent conference in Berlin, dealing just with garlic, presented data on new and novel modes of action for garlic, as well as details on its pharmacological properties, its clinical activities, and its importance in cardiovascular medicine.

Lessons From Garlic

Proverbs 25:2 says: "It is the glory of God to conceal things, but the glory of kings is to search things out" (NRSV).

God conceals some things that a king, or in this case scientists, can search out. The health benefits of garlic have been hidden for years. Current research is proving real health benefits. I believe it is God's will for us to discover and use these hidden healing qualities.

Prayer

Jesus, lover of my soul,
You see all hidden needs and hidden benefits.
We ask you to restore our souls;
Let your cleansing, healing grace abound.
Make and keep us pure within.
May the hidden efficaciousness of your gifts
Continue to be discovered,
And used for the benefit of humankind.
Yes, Lord, so let it be! Amen!

Saffron

A Secret Garden

My sweetheart, my bride, is a secret garden, a walled
garden, a private spring; there the plants flourish. They
grow like an orchard of pomegranate trees and bear
the finest fruits. There is no lack of henna and nard, of
saffron, *calamus and cinnamon, of incense of every*
kind. Myrrh and aloes grow there with all the most fra-
grant perfumes. Fountains water the garden, streams
of flowing water....
— Song of Solomon 4:12-15 (TEV)

The Secret Garden, a book by Frances Hodgson Burnett, tells
the story of children finding a hidden, neglected garden. Their diligent work in it restores the garden and restores the health of pam-
pered and spoiled Dickon. Gardening has brought health and happiness to multitudes of people throughout the world who have taken
time to cultivate the soil, plant seeds, harvest the crops, and smell
the flowers.

Solomon, in the text above, tells of a garden filled with fruit
trees and fragrant plants. The most rare of those mentioned is saffron. Saffron is a delicate, little autumn-flowering crocus. It has
been cultivated and valued for more than 3,500 years. It is one of
the plants that can be identified with certainty. Saffron, or *Crocus*
sativus, as we know it today, is without a doubt the same flower
that grew in Solomon's garden.

The flower grows from a bulb, blooms in the autumn, is laven-
der in color, and has a delicate scent. During Bible times, the petals
were placed in fountains and strewn in theaters because of their
wonderful fragrance. In the first century, the historian Pliny tells
us, "Saffron loves to be beaten and trodden under foot, and in fact,
the worse it is treated the better it thrives." This means that the
bulbs were deliberately injured to produce more offsets, as one of
the methods of increase.

Saffron is the most precious and expensive spice in the world. Saffron filaments, the dried stigmas of the saffron flower, are gathered and prepared at great expense. Each flower has only three stigmas, which must be picked by hand. It takes 4,000 flowers to produce one ounce of spice. As well as fragrance and spice, the flower is in demand as a yellow coloring agent. The flower can also be used to produce essential oils which are used for therapeutic purposes. The stigmas, red in color, are like little capsules that enclose the complex chemicals which produce saffron's aroma, flavor, and yellow dye.

For cooking purposes, the saffron stigmas or threads are ground into powder. When the powder reaches a chef, it may be added directly to any recipe. Then immediately the deep yellow dye, the delicate aroma, and the unique flavor are released.

May your secret garden be filled with the uplifting colors and aromas that bring much delight from saffron.

Lessons From Saffron

We can be as precious as saffron, revealing the secrets of our talents for God.

The Lord God planted a garden,
In the first white days of the world,
And He set there an angel warden,
In a garment of light unfurled.
So near to the peace of Heaven,
That the hawk might nest with the wren,
For there in the cool of the even'
God walked with the first of men.
The kiss of the sun for pardon
The son of the birds for mirth,
One is nearer God's heart in a garden,
Than anywhere else on earth.

— Dorothy Frances Gurney

Prayer

We thank you, Lord, for secret gardens, and also for the serendipity of finding one early spring violet or an unexpected jack-in-the-pulpit. Even the very first dandelion after a long cold winter can be delightful. (You know how we can fuss and fuss about the rest of them.)

Guide us in ways that we may creatively share our gardens and garden experiences with others. We pray in the name of the one who went often to the garden of prayer. Amen!

Spices

The Spice Of Life

*The queen of Sheba heard of King Solomon's fame, and she traveled to Jerusalem to test him with difficult questions. She brought with her a large group of attendants, as well as camels loaded with **spices**, jewels, and a large amount of gold ... She said to the king, "What I heard in my own country about you and your wisdom is true! I did not believe what they told me until I came and saw for myself."* — 2 Chronicles 9:1, 5-6 (TEV)

Today it is easy to go to the supermarket and get spices from all over the world. Even the best food supply would be drab without added spices and flavorings. During Bible times, spices were even more in demand because food that quickly would lose its flavor without refrigeration needed the best of spices to be palatable.

Spices played a decisive part through much of history. Some cities became powerful because they were at the center of the spice trade. The vast demand and the vast amount of money put into spices could be compared to the crude oil trade today. When Columbus set sail, he was hoping to find a better trade route to India and the wealth of spices available there. During World War II, East Indian supplies were cut off for much of the United States. Prices sky-rocketed, and even basic pepper was hardly available.

This spice has been identified as the Astragalus plant. This plant produces a precious gum resin which has a variety of uses, including use as a medicine. The desert astragal, as it is known, is native to Palestine. It can be found growing along the shores of the Dead Sea and also near the top of Mount Hermon. It has pretty pea-like blossoms of pale yellow. Because of its thorns, it is a formidable little plant. The whole plant has spines and strong, sharp prickly thorns. The thorns produce the resin during hours of sunshine and it is collected on balls of cotton.

Lessons From Spices

What is the spice of life? What is it that adds zest, palatability, and flavor to the routine of life? Name some people that have added spice to your life, maybe someone who by their sense of humor or story telling ability have brought joy to many people. Again using some "spicy" names, what can you do to tempt the appetite or tickle the palate of someone who needs some zest added to their life?

Prayer

We realize, dear Lord, that life would be very empty without those individuals who are gifted in providing spice to our life. Guide us in our choices of our entertainment, whether it be on radio or television or in the theater. We pray that talented people who are dedicated to you will use their gifts to provide wholesome entertainment. Bless and guide producers, actors, and script writers for your holy purpose. We know that purpose includes sparkling humor and classical drama that enhances life. Lord, while we pray that you will make us more holy, we also pray that we can serve you with our stories and laughter.

And all God's people said, "Wow and Amen!"

Spikenard

She Did A Beautiful Thing

*... While Jesus was eating, a woman came in with an alabaster jar full of a very expensive perfume made of pure **nard**. She broke the jar and poured the perfume on Jesus' head. Some of the people there became angry and said to one another, "What was the use of wasting the perfume? It could have been sold for more than three hundred silver coins and the money given to the poor!" And they criticized her harshly. But Jesus said, "Leave her alone!... She has done a fine and beautiful thing for me ... She did what she could; she poured perfume on my body to prepare it ahead of time for burial."*
— Mark 14:3-6, 8 (TEV)

How extravagant should love be? Should a whole year's wage be emptied out just to provide perfume? This is an example of very extravagant love. Shortly before Jesus was to die for the sins of the world, a lady (John identifies her as one of the Mary's) pours the most expensive perfume available at the time over Jesus. The value of the spikenard used would be equivalent to a year's wage of an average laborer. Today it could represent $20,000 or more. The silver coin, or denarii, represented a little more than a full day's wage. Jesus, who taught us to be frugal in many ways, complimented her. Love is not love if it calculates the cost.

One of the classic stories told by O. Henry demonstrates the extravagance of love. A couple, Della and Jim, were caught in a time of poverty. They were intensely in love. Both had only one unique possession. Della had exquisitely beautiful hair that flowed to her waist. Jim's pride was a gold watch that he had inherited from his father. In order to have a Christmas gift for Jim, the day before Christmas, Della went out and sold her priceless hair for $20 and bought a platinum fob for Jim's prized watch. The story setting is 100 years ago, so the $20 could be multiplied twenty times over today. When they met on Christmas Eve, Jim was startled

to see her short hair. He loved her no less, but then he handed her his gift, a set of very expensive tortoise-shell combs with jeweled edges for her lovely hair. He had sold his prized gold watch to buy the combs. Each had given the other their all, and even with the losses, their love was enhanced. True love is always extravagant.

Jesus, sensing the unconditional completeness of Mary's love, reminded those around that she did what she could, and it was a beautiful thing. In Bible times, when an honored guest arrived, the person was often anointed with a few drops of perfume. In this case, the entire contents, even to the breaking of the container, gave honor to Jesus. In the East there was a custom that if a drinking glass was used for a highly honored guest, the glass was broken so that it would never again be used by a lesser person.

Spikenard, the plant from which the treasured nard comes, is an herb that grows almost exclusively in India, in the Himalayan Mountains at an elevation of 11,000 to 17,000 feet. It has been used by the Hindus as a medicine or perfume from ancient times. The long trip to bring it to Palestine rendered it even more precious. There is a type of spikenard grown in America, but the quality does not compare. The spikenard includes groupings of pink flowers from the plant's spikes. These spikes grow upright in springtime. The hairy stems, when tied together, release the spikenard's lovely perfume.

Three additional references are found in the Bible for spikenard, all in the Song of Solomon. They are Song of Solomon 1:12, 4:13, and 4:14.

Lessons From Spikenard

The Gospel of John portrays the spikenard: "... and the house was filled with the perfume of the ointment." There is an overflowing beauty and contagion that comes from such an act. Everyone present benefited. And also, the whole Church has been blessed and benefited from this incident. If a blossoming wild rose is stepped on and crushed, the fragrance comes out even more and is present on the boot that crushed it. As Christians may we have a life-enhancing aroma.

Prayer

Lord, may fragrance radiate from us
To enhance the lives of those around us.
Forgive us for the unpleasantness,
Maybe even the foul odors, we may be guilty of.
When we walk with you, we believe
The Beauty of Jesus may be seen in us,
And the love of God, like precious perfume,
Will enhance every life that may touch ours.
May our Church be a Church of purest gold,
And a Church whose fragrance attracts the lost.
In Jesus' precious name, we pray. Amen!

Almond

Reading Signs, Buds, Blossoms, And Nuts

*The next day, when Moses went into the Tent, he saw
that Aaron's stick, representing the tribe of Levi, had
sprouted. It had budded, blossomed, and produced ripe
almonds!*   — Numbers 17:8 (TEV)

Almond, meaning in Hebrew to wake or watch, was a most
valued tree of the ancient world. It was valued for its nuts, oil made
from the nuts, and the beauty of its flowers. The nuts are very good
to eat and are used extensively in candies or baking. Since it was
the first of all the trees in the Holy Land to flower, the "wake" or
"watch" definition was appropriate. Blossoms are produced as early
as January.

The almond is also associated with rebirth of life, because the
blossoms burst out from the seemingly dry stems even before the
leaves appear. The prolific blossoms are a delicate white or light
pink, covering the fifteen to thirty-foot high trees completely. In
the summer the fruit appears, looking like a small, dried-up peach.
This dries and splits to release the weak-shelled stone, which contains the almond kernel.

Almonds are mentioned in the Bible as early as Genesis 43:11,
when it is noted that Jacob included almonds in the gift that he
gave in exchange for grain from Egypt at the time of the famine.
Much later, when the people were in the wilderness, the almond
blossom served as a model for the artists ornamenting the golden
candlesticks.

*He made the lampstand of pure gold ... Each of the six
branches had three decorative flowers shaped like almond blossoms with buds and petals. The shaft of the
lampstand had four decorative flowers shaped like almond blossoms with buds and petals.*
       — Exodus 37:17, 19-20 (TEV)

Verse 8 from Numbers 17 refers to the time in the wilderness. There was a dispute about leadership, so each of the twelve tribes had a plain stick with its name on it placed in front of the Ark of the Covenant. The next morning Aaron's stick had blossomed and bore ripe almonds. This confirmed his unique leadership at a time when many were attempting to rebel against Aaron's position.

Lessons From The Almond

How could it be that in one night, a dry almond stick bears buds, blossoms, and almonds? Jesus said in Matthew 19:26, "With men this is impossible, but with God all things are possible" (KJV). Jesus was referring to the rich entering the kingdom of heaven, but the truth is much broader. God continues his purposes through natural growth, which also is a miracle, but sometimes he uses the supernatural to reveal his will.

Prayer

> *Fairest Lord Jesus,*
> *Ruler of all nature,*
> *O thou of God and man the son,*
> *Thee will I cherish,*
> *Thee will I honor, Thou, my soul's glory, joy, and crown.*
>
> *Fair are the meadows,*
> *Fairer still the woodlands,*
> *Robed in the blooming garb of spring:*
> *Jesus is fairer,*
> *Jesus is purer,*
> *Who makes the woeful heart to sing.*
> — Munster Gesangbuch

Thus we pray, dear Lord, as we praise you for your marvelous revelation in almonds and all nature. Amen!

Beans

A Humble Plant For Hungry People

*When David arrived at Mahanaim, he was met by Shobi
... and Machir ... and Barzillai ... They brought bowls,
clay pots, and bedding, and also food for David and
his men: wheat, barley, meal, roasted grain,* **beans,** *peas,
honey, cheese, cream, and some sheep. They knew that
David and his men would get hungry, thirsty, and tired
in the wilderness.*   — 2 Samuel 17:27-29 (TEV)

The verses above describe a marvelous feast that was prepared
for David and his men at a time when they were trying to keep the
kingship in David's hands. A rebellion led by David's son, Absalom,
almost succeeded.

Beans are mentioned only twice in the Bible. The other reference is in Ezekiel 4:9. It is certain, though, that beans were a basic
part of the diet of many people during Bible times. The ancient
historian Pliny mentions beans as well. They have been a basic
food for thousands of years in almost all cultures. One exception is
Egypt, where the priests at one time, felt that they could be defiled
just by handling them. Currently beans are a vital part of the diet of
many in Egypt.

The *Vicia faba* is the variety of bean that was grown in Israel.
It is an annual planted in December. It attains a height of three feet,
has firm grayish-green leaves, and scented pea-shaped blossoms.
These blossoms are creamy white and have a black blotch on the
upright petals. The blossoms appear in February, and at the end of
June the beans are harvested. Surplus beans are fed to horses and
the stalks are fed to the camels.

Some cultures today depend on beans just as other cultures
depend on rice. Certain kinds of beans are among the most nourishing vegetables that can be eaten. Beans also have the power to
enrich the soil with nitrogen as they grow.

Soy beans, which once were mainly a food for livestock, have
become an ever-increasing source of high protein food for humans.

A seemingly-limitless supply of byproducts found, and new uses continue to be found. Some uses include soy flour, adhesives, linoleum backing, marshmallows, and even chemicals used in fire extinguishers.

In ancient times beans were sometimes used in collecting votes from people. A white bean was a yes vote, a black bean was a no vote. Sometimes election of officials was decided by casting beans.

Lessons From Beans

Aesop, the ancient writer of *Aesop's Fables* fame, wrote in his fable "The Town Mouse and the Country Mouse": "Better beans and bacon in peace than cakes and ale in fear."

This ties in well with some of the biblical Proverbs:

> *Better is a dinner of herbs where love is than a fatted ox and hatred with it* (15:17 RSV). *Better is a little with righteousness than great revenues with injustice* (16:8 RSV). *Better is a dry morsel with quiet than a house full of feasting with strife* (17:1 RSV).

A meal of beans would be a simple meal, but a meal of nourishment. If shared with gratitude, it can be fully satisfying to body and soul.

Prayer

Help us, dear Lord, to remember to give you thanks for every meal, for every bit of nourishment you provide. Forgive us for taking for granted the over-abundant food supply we have here. Instead of longing for exotic food or famous eating places, help us to be content with more simple fare. And as we eat more simply, help us to share our abundance with others.

Open our hearts to provide for those who seldom if ever are fully satisfied with a full stomach and a festive meal. May our hands be your hands in serving others and doing your work today.

We pray in the name of the one who said, "Truly I tell you, just as you did it to one of the least of these who are members of my family, you did it to me" (Matthew 25:40 NRSV). Amen!

Cucumber

For The Dry Soul

*... And the children of Israel also wept again, and said,
Who shall give us flesh to eat? We remember the fish
which we did eat in Egypt freely; the **cucumbers**, and
the melons, and the leeks, and the onions, and the garlic. But now our soul is dried away: there is nothing at
all, besides this manna....* — Numbers 11:4-6 (KJV)

Are cucumbers really good? They are not one of my favorites.
Given the circumstances of the Israelites in the desert in the heat of
summer, however, they surely remembered the refreshing taste of
the garden produce of Egypt. And remembering this, their strength
dried away.

My strength is renewed from the memories I have of picking
fruit from the trees on our farm, including wild plums, wild grapes,
mulberries, and apples. Even with the ample diet I enjoy today, the
memory of those refreshing fruits pulls at my heart. It would be
wonderful to experience that again!

For the Israelites wandering in the wilderness with only a diet
of manna, the longing for something different was almost more
than they could bear. A cool, raw cucumber would have been real
refreshment. And perhaps the Egyptians made other refreshing food,
as we do today, with a vast variety of pickles and relishes.

Cucumber is used only two times in the Bible. The second use
is found in Isaiah: "Jerusalem alone is left, a city under siege — as
defenseless as a watchman's hut in a vineyard or a shed in a cucumber field" (Isaiah 1:8 TEV). As the cucumbers and other produce ripened, a crude shed would be built for storing the produce.
A boy or older man would be responsible to keep thieves and preda-
tors away.

A dry soul can be inferred in Psalm 106: "They were filled
with craving in the desert and put God to the test; so he gave them
what they asked for, but also sent a terrible disease [leanness] among
them" (Psalm 106:14-15 TEV).

Scott Patton

The Israelites had a craving that came between them and God, bringing "leanness," as some translations have it. We, also, are in danger of allowing our craving for material things to bring dryness and leanness to our souls. This is the time to be cool like a cucumber, but not to crave and yearn for it.

The cucumber today is similar to those of Bible times and can be grown where any type of vegetable can be grown. They rank amongst the oldest known vegetables. The color is a rich blue-green, and the flowers are white to light yellow. The vines grow rapidly, producing many branches. If there is a fence or trellis close, the plant will grow on to it. The cucumber may be as little as one inch long or as long as three feet.

Lessons From The Cucumber

The Bible uses the cucumber as a symbol of an unhealthy craving and hunger for satisfaction that comes from things God does not supply. Manna or the Bread of Life that Jesus supplies is that which satisfies the soul. Hunger and thirst for righteousness, and you will be satisfied.

Prayer

Lord, help us to realize
That dryness of the soul
Is the worst kind of dryness.
We confess that we also have
Longed for the "flesh pots" of Egypt.
We have desired material things,
And material does not fill our emptiness.
Gracious Lord, we ask for your forgiveness.
May we allow you to direct our appetites,
So that we might hunger and thirst for righteousness.
Thank you for providing for our appetites and longing
In a most satisfying way.
I am satisfied with Jesus! Amen!

Lentils

Feed Me, I Pray

*Once when Jacob was cooking a stew, Esau came in from the field, and he was famished. Esau said to Jacob, "Let me eat some of that red stuff, for I am famished!" ... Jacob said, "First sell me your birthright." Esau said, "I am about to die; of what use is the birthright to me?" Jacob said, "Swear to me first." So he swore to him, and sold his birthright to Jacob. Then Jacob gave Esau bread and **lentil** stew, and he ate and drank, and rose and went his way. Thus Esau despised his birthright.*
— Genesis 25:29-34 (NRSV)

Although they were twins, Esau was the firstborn, and had the privilege of the birthright, which was very important at that time. It meant that the eldest son succeeded to the official authority of the father, and he received a "double portion" of the paternal property (see Deuteronomy 21:15-17). It also included a special blessing from the father. The biblical writer pointed out how Esau scorned his birthright. Later in their lives, Jacob, with the support of his mother, tricked his father Isaac into giving the blessing of the firstborn to him.

When Esau said, "Feed me, I pray ..." (Genesis 25:30 KJV), he was giving an indication of priorities in his life. In effect he was saying: "Blessings are of little importance; food is what I need and pray for."

Lentils were an important food throughout Bible times. They are among the most nutritious of legumes. Rich and poor alike found it a favorite food for making into soup and stew and baking into bread. Today it is available as a food high in protein and carbohydrates, but low in fat, and is especially attractive for vegetarians.

Lentils belong to the leguminous family of plants. Like the pea, lentils have long pods. The seeds, red-brown in color and about half-inch in diameter, are used as food. The seed splits into two hemispheres, each looking just like a lens. The word "lens" itself was named because a lens looked like a lentil seed.

114

The lentil plant is about eighteen inches in height. It has delicate pinnate leaves terminating in tendrils. The small flowers are white, pale blue, or lilac colored. A further value of the lentil is its ability to grow on unproductive ground. The plant, after the lentil seeds are harvested, is used for fodder for livestock.

Besides the one referred to, the Bible uses "lentil" only two other times: 2 Samuel 17:28 and 23:11.

Lessons From Lentils

The eyes of Esau were blind to family and spiritual values as evidenced by his selling his birthright for a pot of stew. Ask God to sharpen your spiritual insight, so you can choose the values and blessings that last forever. What does having a "birthright" from God mean to you?

Prayer

God of our fathers, and the fathers of our faith, thank you for the biblical record of Abraham, Isaac, Jacob, and their descendants. When we pray, "Give us this day, our daily bread," may we never become so dependent on bread and other material things that they become the center of our prayers.

As we live in a land of overflowing plenty, keep centered in our concerns and prayers the needs of those parts of the world where starvation continues to destroy lives. May the arms of all charities, including the food programs of governments, reach around the world to supply the hungry of all ages, especially children, with adequate food. Amen!

In the name of him who said, "In as much as you have done it unto one of the least of these, you have done it unto me," even our Lord Jesus. Amen.

Mallow

Food For A Famine

(Job is mocked and hated.) *"But now they make sport of me, men who are younger than I ... What could I gain from the strength of their hands, men whose vigor is gone? Through want and hard hunger they gnaw the dry and desolate ground; they pick **mallow** and the leaves of bushes, and to warm themselves the roots of the broom."* — Job 30:1-4 (RSV)

Job's troubles continue. Even those who were far below him in social standing, people who faced the worst kinds of poverty, now were above him in terms of acceptance and standing in the community. There is something about humanity that tries to bring down to our level a consistent winner. Until testing struck him, Job had been a winner. He had been a truly noble man and a man of honestly-earned wealth. Now that was gone, and most others gloated over his demise.

The verses above bring to mind the food that those in poverty might be forced to eat just to survive. The mallow is a large family of plants, and this particular mallow provided an inferior quality of nourishment from its leaves and sometimes the roots. It is a bush that thrives with sea air. It grows abundantly along the shores of southern Europe and along the shores of the Dead Sea.

Mallow has a tiny purple flower that is attached directly to the stem. Despite the unpleasant salty taste, the thick fleshy leaves can be eaten in times of dire necessity. Some today call it the "salt plant," and it may be gathered from many growing places in the wild. There is only one other reference to mallow. It is in Job 24:24 (RSV).

Authorities do not agree on the specific mallow referred to in the Bible. *Pellukhiyeh* is the plant I am referring to. *Mallukh* is another possibility; it refers to the sea purslane. It is a perennnial shrub that grows in the salt marshes. It could be used as a cooked vegetable but only the poorest of families would use it because the leaves are sour.

All together the mallow family of plants includes over 1,000 kinds of herbs, shrubs, and trees. Generally, they are known to have fibrous stems and sticky sap. A few well-known mallow plants include hollyhock, hibiscus, okra, and marshmallow. Another branch of the family includes kola nuts, chocolate, and coca. Yes, the marshmallow, as we know it today, began when the creamy confection from the roots of the mallow, that grows in marshes, was eaten as a sweet delicacy. Today marshmallows do not contain any of the confection of the marsh mallow, but mainly syrups puffed in the packaged form we can buy.

From Finland comes a poem story about "Paavo the Yeoman," written by Johan Ludwig Huneberg. Paavo, in his poverty, depended on finely ground tree bark being added to the flour to have food through the winter. The poem begins by telling how again and again the rye crop has failed because of frost, hail, or flood, and after another failure his wife cries:

"Paavo, Paavo, born a luckless yeoman,
Let us die, for us has God forsaken.
Hard is death, but life is even harder."
Paavo took her hand and spoke, assuring;
"God but tries us, He does not forsake us
Mix thou bark in two-fold with thy flour;
Two-fold larger shall I dig the ditches;
Yet in the Lord I'll put my hope of harvest," ...
So came spring and drift from field was melted,
Still no sprouting crop went floating with it.
And when summer brought the driving hailstorm,
Not by it were stalks beat low and broken.
Autumn came and frost, far from the rye field,
Let the crop stand golden for the reaper.
Then fell Paavo to his knees, thanksgiving;
"God but tries us, He does not forsake us."
And his wife upon her knees repeated:
"God but tries us, He does not forsake us."
But with gladness cried she to her husband;
"Paavo, Paavo, swing with joy the sickle!
Now has come the time for happy living;
Now the time to cast away the birch-bark;

119

Now to bake our bread of rye unblended."
Paavo took her hand and spoke reproving:
"Woman, woman — he stands well the trial —
Who forsakes not then his need-pressed brother.
Mix thou half-part bark in with thy flour —
For in the field our neighbor's crop stands frozen."

Are we a luckless people, or do we survive with mallow, food for a famine, and God's love?

Lessons From Mallow

Though far from a taste delight, the mallow supplied a basic food. While writing this book in the midst of winter, I am always amazed at how God provides food for sparrows, crows, and other wildlife. Their large numbers devour vast amounts of food. They usually eat simply, but they survive. God's feeding of the sparrows reminds us that food, like mallow, helps us survive for him.

Prayer

Loving Lord, we thank you for providing food for life throughout the world. We pray for those who in the midst of poverty must resort to eating insects, the bark of trees, or some tasteless plants just to survive. Guide us to support the causes of charity that best minister to these needs. Amen!

Pistachio Nuts

A Worthy Present

*Their father said to them, "... take the best products of the land in your packs as a present to the governor: a little resin, a little honey, spices, **pistachio nuts**, and almonds."* — Genesis 43:11 (TEV)

Although most Bible translations don't include the word *pistachio*, there is agreement that pistachio is the nut referred to in Genesis 43:11. The verse is a part of the instructions of Father Jacob (Israel) to his eleven sons when they went to Egypt to get grain during a time of famine. At that time pistachio nuts were grown in Israel and throughout Syria but in few other places. Pistachio nuts were a prized possession or gift.

The pistachio tree grows well in dry regions. Even in the time of drought and famine that Genesis 43 refers to, it would have been producing food. The tree grows to a height of thirty feet. The bark is russet in color, and the thick gray-green leaves are winged in shape. The small, soft, pink-colored flowers grow in large bunches from the branches. When the flowers wither, the nuts form in large clusters.

The nuts are oval and have a double shell. The outer shell is mostly red. The inner shell is pale green and tends to open at the edge much like the shell of an oyster. When removed, the esteemed and tasty nut may be eaten or ground and used as a flavoring and coloring for ice cream or candy. The kernels can be salted in brine while still in the shell.

Every pistachio tree is either male or female. In order to produce nuts, the female trees must have a male tree nearby to provide pollen for their flowers. The pistachio belongs to the cashew family. The kernels can be pressed for oil, which is used as a cooking oil or in making varnishes or turpentine.

Scott Potter

Lessons From Pistachio Nuts

There is something very delightful about opening a flavorful nut that has been protected and hidden from sight by the shell. We can learn to take delight in simple things: the smile of a friend, the discovery of spring's first flowers, and the opening of a nut that human eyes have never seen before!

Prayer

Thank you, Lord, for the flavorful taste of nuts.
There is no end to the variety of textures and tastes we enjoy.
Bless the world service projects of all denominations and in
     all countries.
May the planting of trees, the distribution of seeds,
The giving of animals through the Heifer Project
Help bring the blessing of a healthy diet to all people.
We offer this prayer in the loving name of Jesus. Amen!

Wheat

Yielding One Hundredfold

> *His pleasure is not in strong horses, nor his delight in brave soldiers; but he takes pleasure in those who honor him, in those who trust his constant love ... He keeps your gates strong; he blesses your people. He keeps your borders safe and satisfies you with the finest **wheat**.*
> — Psalm 147:10-11, 13-14 (TEV)

For over 9,000 years wheat has been cultivated by humankind. It was instrumental in changing early humanity. As humans evolved from hunters, with no permanent homes, to farmers with more permanent homes, they could now raise the grain they needed for food and store it for use in the winter. Wheat that is about 3,000 years old has been found in some of the Egyptian pyramids. When planted, some of this ancient wheat grew. Imagine the monumental amount of grain that could have grown from the wheat, if each year it had been planted.

Wheat is the world's most important grain crop. It is a very nourishing food source, being made up of twelve percent protein, seventy percent carbohydrates, two percent fat, and nearly two percent minerals. The whole wheat, including the bran coating, is one of the most complete natural foods available.

No wonder Jesus said:

> *"I am telling you the truth, what Moses gave you was not the bread from heaven; it is my Father who gives you the real bread from heaven. For the bread that God gives is he who comes down from heaven and gives life to the world ... I am the bread of life ... He who comes to me will never be hungry; he who believes in me will never be thirsty."* — John 6:32-33, 35 (TEV)

In the parable of the sower Jesus told about the seed falling in difficult areas and yielding little, but some fell in good soil and

produced a hundredfold (Luke 8:4-8). As the artist has pictured here, the variety of wheat Jesus has in mind is *Triticum compositum*. Instead of just one spike or ear of grain, it produces seven, and could well have one hundred or more kernels of wheat. Jesus made reference to an abundant yield that good soil would produce. With proper care, wheat brings a generous return. Worldwide, wheat harvested is about 590 million metric tons, which is over twenty billion bushels. In the United States alone, each person annually consumes about 120 pounds of wheat in breads, cereals, cakes, and a multitude of other wheat-based food.

The word *wheat* is used 51 times in the Bible. One of the passages that does not include "wheat," but definitely refers to it, is Genesis 41:5. The King James Version uses the term "ears of corn" in telling of the dream of Pharaoh, which Joseph was able to interpret. The grain on the stalk is variously known as head, ear, spike, or sheaf. Most plants of wheat grow only one spike. The plant itself is grass-like, growing two to five feet in height, terminating in the grain-bearing head. When the grain ripens, it turns into an appealing golden brown.

In Bible times and up until the invention of the McCormick reaper in the nineteenth century, harvesting was done by cutting the wheat down with sharp sickles. Then it was gathered into bundles for further drying. Threshing was done by beating with special clubs, or by slapping the grain heads against rocks. Winnowing was done by tossing the grain into the air against the wind; then it would be sieved into large heaps. Usually a watchman would sleep by the mounds of winnowed wheat to protect them from thieves or pests. In most parts of the world today, that whole process is done with speed and efficiency by self-propelled combines. One person is now able to do what once took up to 500 people to do.

Special festive events were planned for the Jewish people surrounding the time of the wheat harvest. The main festival was the Feast of Weeks (Exodus 34:22). Biblical references also talk about harvesting (Ruth 2:23); threshing (Judges 6:11); cleaning (2 Samuel 4:6); and winnowing (Matthew 3:12).

Lessons From Wheat

If we accept Jesus as the Bread of Life, we find that the deepest hungers of our human hearts are satisfied. Think about what you have eaten in the past week. How many things did you eat that did not contain wheat flour in any form? Basic to our sacrificial Christian teaching is: "A grain of wheat, unless it die, can never, never multiply." The seed sacrifices its life so new life can develop.

Prayer

> Thank you, Dear Lord, for taking pleasure in those who honor you,
> In those who trust in your constant love!
> Even if terrorists strike, you keep our borders safe.
> You satisfy us with the finest wheat.
> You provide us with a vast storehouse of splendid food.
> Amen!

Aloe

The Oil Of Gladness

*How goodly are thy ... tabernacles, O Israel! As the
valleys are they spread forth, as gardens by the river's
side, as the trees of **aloes** which the Lord hath planted....*
— Numbers 24:5-6 (KJV)

*You love righteousness ... therefore God, your God, has
anointed you with the oil of gladness beyond your com-
panions; your robes are all fragrant with myrrh and
aloes and cassia. From ivory palaces stringed instruments make you glad....* — Psalm 45:7-8 (NRSV)

There are two kinds of aloe as presented in the Bible. The above
passages refer to a large tree that was highly prized for the wood
and the fragrant aloe. In the center of its inner trunk is found a
dark-colored fragrant substance, a priceless perfume. Also the fragrant inner wood was used for a setting for precious stones and
was considered worth its weight in gold. A popular belief in the
East is that this is the only plant that survived from the Garden of
Eden, which was planted by God. The aloe was brought out of the
garden by Adam, and the belief is that from this one all aloe trees
have come. To this day it is called "Paradise Wood."

The verses above contain favorite phrases for poets and
songwriters. The Garden of Eden was planted by God in a unique
way, but it is true that every tree grows by the hand of God. And he
is involved in every growing thing. The oil of gladness, in the con-
text of Psalm 45, refers to the perfumed anointing oils that were so
basic and important to the culture of that time. Oil was used by the
Jews for anointing the body after a bath, and there were certain oils
that only the rich could afford. Psalm 45 is actually a royal wedding song and it refers to the finest, most royal part of the palace.

How wonderfully true it is that God's touch can bring gladness
to our lives. Like the perfumed oil, there is a special beauty and
special fragrance for our spiritual lives.

The hymn writer, Henry Barraclaugh, portrays Psalm 45 in his hymn, "Out Of The Ivory Palaces":

My Lord has garments so wondrous fine,
And myrrh their texture fills;
Its fragrance reached to this heart of mine,
With joy my being thrills.

Out of the ivory palaces, into a world of woe,
Only His great, eternal love made my Savior go.
His life had also its sorrows sore,
For aloes had a part;
And when I think of the cross He bore,
My eyes with tear drops start.

His garments too were in cassia dipped,
With healing in a touch;
Each time my feet in some sin have slipped,
He took me from its clutch.

In garments glorious He will come,
To open wide the door;
And I shall enter my heavenly home,
To dwell forever more.

Aloe, when referred to in the New Testament, is a different plant than those of the Old Testament. It is a handsome, succulent plant. In some ways it is similar in appearance to the aloe vera plant. The thick, fleshy, lance-shaped leaves grow from a heavy rosette just above the root. From the center of this cluster grows a stalked flower head. The flowers are bell-shaped and about two inches long. These flowers open progressively from the base of the spike. Colors range from bright vermilion to yellow.

The juice obtained from the thick leaves of this succulent plant is dissolved in water and added to sweet-smelling incenses. It was used in purifying the bodies of the dead.

... Joseph of Arimathea ... and ... Nicodemus ... brought
a mixture of myrrh and aloes, about an hundred pound

weight. Then took they the body of Jesus, and wound it in linen clothes with the spices, as the manner of the Jews is to bury. — John 19:38-40 (KJV)

Lessons From The Aloe

Many people keep an aloe vera plant growing in their kitchen to have a ready supply of liquid from the leaves as a burn remedy. The remedy for spiritual pain can be the "oil of gladness," freely offered to us as a part of God's love. When many others had forsaken him, Joseph and Nicodemus risked being identified with Jesus when they provided a dignified burial for him.

Prayer

Lord Jesus, we long to be perfectly whole. Even before modern medicine, you supplied remedies for the sickness and pain that are a part of life. We pray that modern medicine can use the best of drug therapy as well as the best of natural remedies to meet the needs of this day. Guide and bless those who work in research to develop new medicines. We pray that soon a reliable remedy may be found for illnesses, such as cancer, just as in the past remedies have been found for polio and smallpox. May those who work for medical solutions know that you work shoulder-to-shoulder with them in restoration of health. We pray in the name of Jesus, the Great Physician. Amen!

Balm

For Great Pain, A Great Balm

*"Is there no **balm** in Gilead? Is there no physician there?*
Why then has the health of my poor people not been
restored?"   — Jeremiah 8:22 (NRSV)

Several different plants have been called "balm." Specifically for our purpose here, we are identifying the balm of Gilead, a small evergreen tree, that was abundant in parts of Palestine. From the sap of this plant is obtained a resinous substance. Since ancient times, this sap has been valued for its fragrance and healing properties. Gum resin from the bark is still deemed to have healing properties. Until the seventeenth century, it was the ingredient in many medicines.

The balm grows twelve to fourteen feet in height, and has a delicate white blossom that turns into a deep purple, plum-like fruit. These are picked before they ripen, and rich oil is extracted. This oil is very fragrant and is valued for healing properties.

The prophet Jeremiah advises failing Babylon: "Bring balm for her wound; perhaps she may be healed" (Jeremiah 51:8 NRSV).

Several other biblical passages speak of balm as a valued gift and as a basic part of provisions. When Joseph was in Egypt and the brothers tried to gain his favor, they included balm as one of their gifts:

> *Then their father Israel said to them ... "take some of*
> *the choice fruits of the land in your bags, and carry*
> *them down as a present to the man — a little balm and*
> *a little honey, gum, resin, pistachio nuts, and almonds."*
>   — Genesis 43:11 (NRSV)

Healing is also referred to in Jeremiah:

> *Go up to Gilead and take balm, O virgin daughter of*
> *Egypt! In vain you have used many medicines; there is*
> *no healing for you.*   — Jeremiah 46:11 (RSV)

I am reminded of the old spiritual:

"There is a balm in Gilead to make the wounded whole;
There is a balm in Gilead to heal the sin sick soul."

Another type of balm plant, now grown in the United States, is a tall fragrant herb of the mint family. It is used for seasoning, and a tea is made from the leaves to help reduce fever.

Lessons From The Balm

The dictionary includes synonyms for balm: "solace, comfort, and consolation." A quote from William C. Bryant refers to the balm for rest and sleep.

In our weariness we can come to God and find him as hope, help, and balm. Where there are wounds around us, whether physical, mental, or spiritual, we are called to the task of providing the balm of healing.

Prayer

Lord Jesus, so many, many times you have been balm for our weariness. Again and again we need to hear your words:

Come unto me all ye that labor and are heavy laden
and I will give you rest. Take my yoke upon you and
learn of me ... For my yoke is easy and my burden is
light. — Matthew 11:28-30 (KJV)

So guide us to be balm for those around us who are weary. May we recognize those places in our communities and throughout the world that are most in need of your healing balm, and reach out to help them. In Jesus' name. Amen!

Hemlock

Death Be Not Proud

*Israel is an empty vine ... Their heart is divided ... They have spoken words, swearing falsely in making a covenant: thus judgment springeth up as **hemlock** in the furrows of the field.* — Hosea 10:1, 2, 4 (KJV)

Hosea preached in the northern kingdom of Israel during very troubled times. He was especially concerned about idolatry and the faithlessness of the people towards God. In the verse above, Hosea is talking about the Lord's judgment on Israel.

Hemlock refers both to a beautiful coniferous evergreen tree and to a poisonous herb belonging to the parsley family. For our purpose here, we refer to the poison hemlock. Many in past generations used it to murder or commit suicide. Poison hemlock was used to put Socrates to death. Among ancient Athenians it was given to prisoners who had been given the death penalty.

The plant has finely cut dark-green leaves resembling a fern. At the top of the branching stems are small white flowers grouped into flat-topped clusters called umbels. The plant may attain a height of five feet. All parts of the hemlock plant, particularly the seeds, contain an oily substance known as caria. If taken internally, it brings on paralysis, convulsions, and even death.

In the Old Testament the prophet Amos, warning of the destruction of Israel, says: "... for ye have turned judgment into gall, and the fruit of righteousness into hemlock" (Amos 6:12 KJV).

Another translation puts it this way: "You have turned justice into poison, and right into wrong" (TEV). What a terrible truth to have leveled at a nation.

The theme for this devotional thought is: "Death be not proud," which is a quotation from John Donne's sonnet titled "Death." A little later in the sonnet Donne shares his faith: "One short sleep past, we wake eternally; And death shall be no more; death, thou shalt die." Because of Jesus we claim that truth.

135

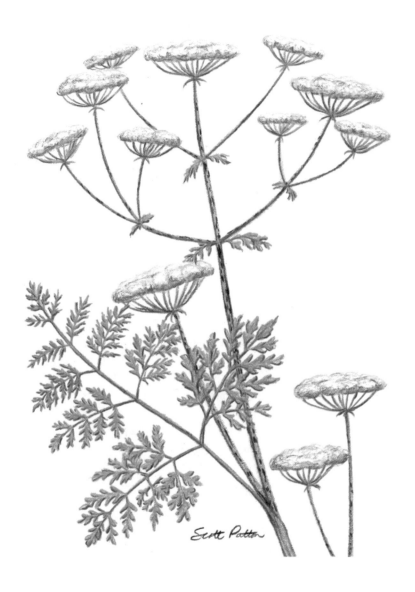

Death is a reality. I have said a final farewell to parents, grandparents, and many friends. As a pastor I have officiated at hundreds of funerals. For some, death can come as a welcome relief after a full and good life. For others, it rips apart life's closest bonds, and leaves hearts broken and lonely. Because of Jesus, we know death does not have the last word. He has brought about the death of death.

1 Corinthians 15:26 says: "The last enemy to be destroyed is death." Paul continues:

> *When this perishable body puts on imperishability, and this mortal body puts on immortality, then the saying that is written will be fulfilled:*
> *"Death has been swallowed up in victory.*
> *Where, O death, is your victory?*
> *Where, O death, is your sting?"*
> *The sting of death is sin, and the power of sin is the law. But thanks be to God, who gives us the victory through our Lord Jesus Christ.*
> — 1 Corinthians 15:54-57 (NRSV)

Lessons From Hemlock

Just as hemlock can bring physical death and is to be avoided, so also anything that may bring spiritual death is to be avoided. Hosea and Amos plead with their people to return to God. For the most part, the warning was not followed, and the death or captivity of the nation was the result. Make a list of secret, possibly masquerading things, that can bring physical or spiritual death.

Prayer

Source of life and love,
We follow and praise you,
The Way, the Truth and the Life!
Sometimes we have poisoned ourselves
With improper diets,
Or poisonous thoughts and attitudes.
Even worse and more direct,
We consume alcohol, nicotine,

137

And mood-altering drugs.
Forgive us for all destructive
Habits and attitudes.
Give us the courage to say, "No!"
To any and every poison
We may be tempted to consume;
Or even the poison thoughts,
That can pollute our mind and soul.
Cleanse and purify us with the Living Water,
Quench our thirst with your bountiful supply.
May our remembrance of the waters of Baptism,
Renew and revive us.
Feed and nourish us with the Bread of Life.
In Jesus' life-giving name we pray. Amen!

Mandrake

Birth As A Gift

*But Rachel had not borne Jacob any children, and so she became jealous of her sister ... During the wheat harvest Reuben went into the fields and found **mandrakes**, which he brought to his mother Leah. Rachel said to Leah, "Please give me some of your son's **mandrakes."** ... Then God remembered Rachel; he answered her prayer ... She became pregnant and gave birth to a son ... so she named him Joseph.*
— Genesis 30:1, 14, 22-24 (TEV)

The Israelites believed that children were truly a gift of God. If children were not born, it was because God had shut the womb (1 Samuel 1:5-6). If children were born, it was because God had opened the womb (Genesis 29:31). Although they prayed to God for his gift of life, they were not beyond using other methods to help with the pregnancy.

There was a strong belief that mandrakes would help a woman become pregnant. Except for one reference in the Song of Solomon, all references in the Bible to mandrakes are found in Genesis chapter 30, part of which is quoted above.

People have long held superstitions about the mandrake, based in part on the fact that its forked root bears some resemblance to the human figure. Superstitions include beliefs that the mandrake brought good luck, induced fertility, was a charm against evil spirits, helped discover treasure, and was a powerful "love potion."

There is evidence that this was not all superstition. A dose of the oddly shaped root was sometimes given to patients as a narcotic or anesthetic and was somewhat effective for that purpose. It is also used as an aphrodisiac in some cultures even today.

The plant can be cultivated but grows wild in Europe and Asia. The plant has no stem, and the leaves grow directly from the root. The leaves are large, nearly a foot long, and resemble spinach. The flowers (that do have a stem) are cup-shaped. They are creamy

yellow in color with purple veins. It bears a small red fruit shaped like a tomato. The fruit has a strong smell, but many people develop an appetite for it and consider it a health-enhancing delicacy. Were Rachel and Leah foolish to acquire mandrakes to help their fertility problems? Maybe not, I believe God expects us to use the best resources available to help answer prayer. Dwight L. Moody, a great Christian and man of prayer, was asked one time what he would do if his daughter was terribly sick. Would he depend on prayer or would he depend on a doctor? His answer was, "I would pray as if everything depended on prayer, and I would get the very best doctor's care, as if everything depended on the doctor."

Our belief in an omnipotent God does not close the door to other channels of help that may be available. This is not an issue of one belief or another. We pray diligently for mission work, for renewal and revival in the church, and for the needs of children who may be starving. We also put action into our prayers by delivering food to the needy, sending missionaries, and inviting others into the fellowship of Christ and the church.

Lessons From The Mandrake
Reuben, the son of Leah, found some mandrakes growing wild. According to Genesis 30, the history of the Israelites may have been changed drastically if Reuben had not shared this treasured find. Just as life comes as a "gift," there are opportunities each day to see the hand of God providing "gifts" that we can give to bring blessings, maybe even life to others.

Prayer
Gracious God, we have seen how your hand was in the events of the lives of Jacob, Leah, and Rachel. Their children came to them as a gift from you. The twelve sons of Jacob were all instrumental in carrying out your plan and purpose. We see children born today as gifts and blessings and pray with the hymn writer:

Child of love, our love's expression,
love's creation, loved in deed!

Fresh from God, refresh our spirits,
into joy and laughter lead.
Child of joy, our dearest treasure,
God's you are, from God you came.
Back to God we humbly give you;
live as one who bears Christ's name.
Child of God your loving Parent,
learn to know whose child you are.
Grow to laugh and sing and worship,
trust and love God more than all.[1]

We pray in Jesus' name. Amen!

---

1. Ronald S. Cole-Turner, "Child of Blessing, Child of Promise." Used by permission of author.

Myrrh

Suffering Is Coming

*... When they saw the child with his mother Mary, they knelt down and worshiped him. They brought out their gifts of gold, frankincense, and **myrrh**, and presented them to him.* — Matthew 2:11 (TEV)

The word "myrrh" is used seventeen times in the Bible. It may seem to be an ancient term with no application today, but a check of the internet indicated that there are 6,000 places of information on the worldwide web.

Currently myrrh is a common ingredient of toothpowder, and is used with borax in tincture, as a mouthwash. It may be used as a stomach carminative, exciting the appetite and the flow of gastric juice, and as an astringent wash. It is used in veterinary practice for healing wounds. Myrrh has been found to kill cancer cells and may be a powerful helper in the fight to overcome cancer. People promoting natural living and dependence on a natural healing process have found myrrh very effective.

The three gifts brought to Jesus were symbolic of his future: gold (a gift for a king), frankincense (a gift for a priest), and myrrh (a gift for one who is to die). A famous painting by Holman Hunt pictures the sun shining through the open door of a carpenter shop, where Jesus, still a boy, has been working. Jesus stands to stretch in this doorway, and the shadow with his arms stretching is the shadow of a cross.

The gift of myrrh was a reminder. John H. Hopkins writes of these gifts from the Wise Men in "We Three Kings":

Born a King on Bethlehem's plain,
gold I bring to crown him again,
King forever, ceasing never,
over us all to reign.
Frankincense to offer have I;
incense owns a Deity nigh;

143

Prayer and praising, voices raising,
worshiping God on high.
Myrrh is mine; its bitter perfume
breathes a life of gathering gloom;
Sorrowing, sighing, bleeding, dying,
sealed in the stone-cold tomb.
Glorious now behold him arise;
King and God and sacrifice....

The myrrh plant grows up to nine feet tall. The large trunk has many knotted branches. Small trifoliate leaves grow in clusters on the wood. To harvest the valuable resin or gum, the bark is pierced, and a thick white gum appears, which hardens and can be collected. Since earliest times and continuing today, the aromatic resin is gathered and sold as a valuable spice or medicine.

On the night of the crucifixion Nicodemus came:

> *"... and brought a mixture of myrrh and aloes, about*
> *an hundred pound weight. Then took they the body of*
> *Jesus, and wound it in linen clothes with the spices, as*
> *the manner of the Jews is to bury."*
> — John 19:39-40 (KJV)

Lessons From Myrrh

Some age-old remedies are still valuable and usable today. It is amazing that this ancient plant is still in use, and new healing qualities are currently being discovered.

Prayer

Dear Lord Jesus, myrrh is a reminder ...
A reminder of the suffering you endured,
A reminder of the agony of the cross,
A reminder of the real pain and torment you endured.
Help us today to remember those who suffer.
Suffering because of terrorists,
Suffering because of war, land mines, and injustice,
Suffering because of sickness and pain,
Suffering because of sin

As evidenced in cruelty,
Hate, drug addiction, and craving materialism.

Thank you for the teaching of scripture:

> *Dear friends, do not be surprised at the painful test you are suffering ... Rather be glad that you are sharing Christ's suffering, so that you may be full of joy when his glory is revealed ... If you suffer because you are a Christian, don't be ashamed of it, but thank God that you bear Christ's name.*
>
> — 1 Peter 4:12-13, 16 (TEV)

In your name we pray. Amen!

Bulrush

Born For A Purpose

*Then Pharaoh commanded all his people, "Every son
that is born to the Hebrews you shall cast into the Nile,
but you shall let every daughter live." Now a man from
the house of Levi went and took to wife a daughter of
Levi. The woman conceived and bore a son; and when
she saw that he was a goodly child, she hid him three
months. And when she could hide him no longer she
took for him a basket made of bulrushes, and daubed it
with bitumen and pitch; and she put the child in it and
placed it among the reeds at the river's brink.*
— Exodus 1:22; 2:1-3 (RSV)

The bulrush, a bountiful and graceful plant, covers much of the
area along the Nile River's edge. In ancient Egypt the plants were
so prolific that at places it completely covered the surface of the
Nile. It grows to a height of twelve to fifteen feet, with stalks that
are two or three inches in diameter. The stalks bear no foliage. The
heavy sharp-edged leaves grow directly from the rootstock. It has a
heavy root system, important in holding it in place during floods.
The roots were also collected to burn as fuel. At the top of the stock
there is a plume of brown rush-like flowers that produce seeds.

Today the plant is more commonly known as papyrus, and it
provided the earliest known material for making a crude paper.
Paper gets its name from this plant. The paper of ancient Egypt
was made of strips of the stem. The strips were laid in layers and
later placed under heavy pressure. The strips then could be used as
crude porous white paper. For a while the sheets were preserved by
rolling and tying with string. Later they were bound together, similar to modern books.

The bulrushes or papyrus were also used for mats, sandals,
sailcloth, and building material. The earliest paint brushes may have
been made by fraying the ends of the stalks. According to Isaiah
18:2, even boats were made of bulrushes at that time.

147

Scott Patton

As we know from the text given above, the bulrush played a prominent part in the drama to save Moses. An interesting sidenote to crude oil exploration, comes from Exodus 2:1-3: a geologist, when reading the Bible, reasoned that if there were pitch and bitumen present, there had to be petroleum close by, and he was right.

Because of the prolific birthrate among the Children of Israel in Egypt, an attempt was made to control their rapid growth in numbers. Instead of allowing her son to be killed, the mother of Moses risked her life to build him the little "ark." She floated it downstream in hopes that he would be found by some of the royalty. Moses was found, his life was spared, and we remember the rest of the incredible story of God using Moses for his purpose. If the ark made of bulrushes had not been made, these events may never have happened.

Lessons From The Bulrush

The mother of Moses had no resources to save a child. But God directed her to make use of a readily available means of escape. She was faced with an impossible mission. No matter how impossible our mission may be, if we look to God, he will provide the resources, the means of escape, and the means for carrying out a mission of service for others. The history of the Children of Israel, as well as the history of the whole world, has been changed because the mother of Moses used common bulrush reeds. So common for that area, most would have called them weeds.

Prayer

Most gracious God, your plans and purposes are beyond our understanding. Could you actually conquer the power of a great nation and deliver your people from slavery in Egypt because a mother fashioned a boat from bulrushes to save her baby? Yes, dear Lord, that is what you did, and we are amazed. We pray that you will continue to work out your purposes today. Help us to help those who are caught in poverty, meaninglessness, or various kinds of slavery. I pray that you will show me the purpose for my life and strengthen me for service no matter how great the odds. Amen!

Cotton

Queen Of Cloths

*When these days were completed, the king gave for all the people present in Susa, the capital, both great and small, a banquet lasting for seven days, in the court of the garden of the king's palace. There were white **cotton** curtains and blue hangings caught up with cords of fine linen and purple to silver rings and marble pillars....* — Esther 1:5-6 (RSV)

Although the Bible only uses the word "cotton" once, cotton can rightfully be called the "Queen of Cloths." For centuries and centuries cotton has been the main cloth or fiber used by virtually every nation. Even with the introduction of synthetic materials, the use of cotton continues to rise. Currently every person in the United States uses 27 pounds of cotton material per year, up from 22 pounds per person 25 years ago.

It is very possible that the "swaddling cloths" or "bands of cloth" in which Jesus was wrapped, as recorded in Luke 2:7, were made from cotton. It is unlikely that cotton was grown in Palestine at the time of the Old Testament events; linen made from flax and wool were the most common materials. In New Testament times there was widespread use of cotton, even in areas where it was not grown.

Properly woven cotton can be among the softest material in existence. A story in the *Upper Room* told of a man being placed on a cold cart to be taken to surgery. Clad only in a backless hospital gown, he was really cold. Then a caring nurse placed a preheated soft cotton blanket over him, and instead of feeling cold and alone, he felt loved, warmed, and cared for. The dictionary even includes as one of the definitions for cotton: "to get on together, agree, harmonize; to take a liking to."

The use of the word *cotton* in the text above is a part of the descriptive wording in reference to the lavish luxury of the palace of King Ahasuerus. The description continues:

There were ... couches of gold and silver on a mosaic pavement of porphyry, marble, mother-of-pearl and precious stones. Drinks were served in golden goblets, goblets of different kinds.... — Esther 1:6-7 (NRSV)

Read the entire book of Esther (only seven pages), and be inspired again by the daring of Esther and her Uncle Mordecai to save the Jews.

Lessons From Cotton

Cotton is the most common of all fabric material, and perhaps it is the most versatile. It can be dyed with delicate and beautiful colors. It can be used for durable blue denim material or for the softest of materials. So also God calls us to be versatile, as Paul put it once: "I have become all things to all people, that I might by all means save some" (1 Corinthians 9:22 NRSV).

Prayer

Gentle Shepherd,
Much we need thy tender care.
As we have been warmed by your love,
And clothed by your righteousness,
May we be those who reach out in love
To those most in need.
Savior, may we also be as shepherds,
As we meet the lost, the unloved, and the lonely.
We pray in the name of the Gentle Shepherd,
Our Lord Jesus. Amen!

Flax

Our Savior Wrapped In Linen

*When it was evening, there came a rich man from Arimathea, named Joseph, who was also a disciple of Jesus. He went to Pilate and asked for the body of Jesus; then Pilate ordered it to be given to him. So Joseph took the body and wrapped it in a clean **linen** cloth and laid it in his own new tomb, which he had hewn in the rock. He then rolled a great stone to the door of the tomb....* — Matthew 27:57-60 (NRSV)

The word *flax* is used eleven times in the Bible, but the powerful verses above refer to the linen which was made from flax. The word *linen* is used about 100 times. Flax was raised for the very valuable cloth that could be produced from it, and at that time, other than wool, it was the main cloth in use. Although synthetic fibers have taken the place of some linen, flax continues to be grown throughout the world. It is grown for the linen produced and for the seeds of a similar variety of flax used in producing linseed oil and a feed supplement for animals.

Flax grows about 36 inches high and has a beautiful five-petal blue flower. With narrow leaves, the whole plant is rather dainty. In early times the crop was pulled up by its roots and laid out to dry. The stems were soaked in water. The process, called retting, frees the fibers by rotting the woody part of the stock. The next step was to split and comb the fibers until the useful threads separated and peeled off the stalk. A spindle and distaff were used to separate the fine thread, which was then ready to be woven into linen. For the finest linen, finer and finer combs are used, resulting in lace quality linen. The coarse fibers can be made into cord, twines, yarns, and upholstery padding. Egypt was known as the source of the finest linen of the time. Moses spoke of its superior excellence.

The Holy Shroud that Jesus was wrapped in at the time of his burial would have been a very large rectangular-shaped, blanket-like, linen cloth on which he would have been laid. Then the upper

Scott Patton

154

portion would fold down over Jesus' head to reach his feet. Winding cloths were then wrapped around him. Joseph, the man of wealth, would have had access to this high quality burial linen cloth.

One of the fascinating references to flax in the Old Testament is found in Joshua, chapter 2. The spies who had gone to Jericho were in danger of being discovered. Rahab befriended the spies and offered to hide them: "She ... brought them up to the roof and hid them with the stalks of flax that she had laid out on the roof" (Joshua 2:6 NRSV).

They were not found, and safely completed their mission and returned.

> *A capable wife who can find? She is far more precious than jewels.*
> *She seeks wool and flax, and works with willing hands.*
> *She opens her hand to the poor and reaches out her hands to the needy.*
> — Proverbs 31:10, 13, and 20 (NRSV)

Today we can buy fine linen table cloths, handkerchiefs, and a great variety of linen items very reasonably. At the time of the writing of Proverbs, it was a difficult task. No wonder the capable wife would get up before daylight to do her round of demanding activities. Linen is also given a place in the heavenly vision of John.

> *To her it has been granted to be clothed with fine linen, bright and pure — for the fine linen is the righteous deeds of the saints.*
> *And the armies of heaven, wearing fine linen, white and pure, were following him on white horses.*
> — Revelation 19:8, 14 (NRSV)

Lessons From Flax
The ancient method of processing flax into linen took about eighteen months. A new continuous system reduced the time to ten days. That process though has not diminished the quality or the need for waiting patiently while the seeds germinate and the plants grow. Very careful work can bring the finest beauty of lace work or

155

fine clothing. We are called to "wait for the Lord." So also waiting and working can produce enduring, useful, and beautiful handwork.

Prayer

Gracious Lord,
We desire to be pure.
Let your healing, cleansing fountain flow.
Wash away our sins just now.
As we receive your forgiveness,
We want to be those who freely offer forgiveness to others.
If I have wounded any soul today,
Dear Lord, forgive me.
Amen!

Gourd

For Shade Or For Shame?

> *So Jonah went out of the city, and sat on the east side of
> the city, and there made him a booth, and sat under it
> in the shadow, till he might see what would become of
> the city. And the Lord God prepared a **gourd**, and made
> it to come up over Jonah, that it might be a shadow
> over his head, to deliver him from his grief. So Jonah
> was exceedingly glad of the **gourd**. But God prepared
> a worm when the morning rose the next day, and it smote
> the **gourd** that it withered.* — Jonah 4:5-7 (KJV)

Jonah had a lot of potential, but also a lot of trouble brought on
by his own selfishness and prejudice. God had called him to preach
to the city of Nineveh, the capital of the ancient empire of Assyria,
which often had been an enemy of the Jewish nation. Jonah disobeyed, trying to get away on a boat going the opposite direction.
That gave occasion to his being thrown overboard and then swal-
lowed and saved by the great fish. He finally did preach to Nineveh,
and the people believed his message, repented, and turned to God.
Jonah then, instead of rejoicing in a spiritual victory, grumbled
about God's goodness and mercy. He was angry seeing that the
people of Nineveh were spared. So Jonah stayed for a while on the
edge of the city grumbling about the heat. God prepared a plant, a
"gourd," to provide shade. Quickly it had grown, then quickly it
died, and again Jonah was angry. Then the Lord said to him:

> *"... This plant grew up in one night and disappeared
> the next; you didn't do anything for it ... yet you feel
> sorry for it! How much more, then, should I have pity
> on Nineveh, that great city."* — Jonah 4:10-11 (TEV)

The Bible uses *gourd* for two different kinds of plants. The
term in Jonah refers to what is also called the castor bean plant.
The castor plant may be ten feet tall, grows quickly, but if handled

Scott Potter

or disturbed also wilts quickly. It has large broad leaves providing good shade. The flowers are vermilion colored with tiny sepals, among rich cream-colored anthers.

The vining gourd, with which we are most familiar, was also grown throughout Bible times. Gourds are vegetables closely related to squashes and pumpkins. 1 Kings 6:18 and 7:24 tell of the gourd motifs that decorated the temple interior. Gourds grow very rapidly and bear fruits of various sizes and color. They are easy to grow, and through many centuries have had multiple uses. Some of them are suitable for cups, utensils, or storage vessels. They also make suitable bird houses.

Lessons From The Gourd

Jonah learned something about obedience and the mercy of God. God reminded him that the people and children of Nineveh, whom he had created and loved, were much more important than the plant that grew to provide shelter for him. All people of all nationalities are included in God's love, and we are called to share the love of God with them.

Prayer

O Lord our Lord,
You have a plan for every person
And every nation.
Often we have been disobedient
To your call and to
The heavenly vision.
We have been comfortable caring for our own.

Bless us with hearts of caring concern
As we reach out in your name
To lift and love others. Amen!

Olive

Give Me Oil In My Lamp

*I am like an **olive** tree growing in the house of God; I trust in his constant love forever and ever. I will always thank you, God, for what you have done; in the presence of your people I will proclaim that you are good.*
— Psalm 52:8-9 (TEV)

In Bible times the olive was the most important tree in the area. It was a good symbol of trust in and love for God. Olive trees live a long time, and when cut down can sprout from the root. They have a foundation of firm roots. The uses of the tree and its fruit touched almost every phase of daily life, including food, fuel, light, carpentry, ointments, and medicines. In Deuteronomy 6:11, the olive tree is included in the things that were promised to be a part of the glory of the Promised Land.

The olive produces an abundance of oil. One olive tree could produce half a ton of oil each year. This was enough to provide a whole family with all the oil needed for cooking and for a butter-like spread. The seed does not contain oil, but up to thirty percent of the content of the fruit is oil. Although having a high fat content, olive oil is one of the healthiest for human consumption.

"Give me oil in my lamp," could well have been the concern of Aaron as mentioned in Leviticus 24:

... bring pure olive oil of the finest quality for the lamps in the Tent, so that a light might be kept burning regularly ... Aaron shall take care of the lamps on the lampstand of pure gold and must see that they burn regularly in the Lord's presence.
— Leviticus 24:2, 4 (TEV)

The oil was vital for many types of cooking or baking. 1 Kings 17:12 tells about the widow Elijah was sent to see, who said she had nothing to eat but "a handful of flour in a bowl and a bit of

Scott Patton

olive oil in a jar." Also, olive oil has been recognized as having healing qualities, and some use it for anointing (James 5:14).

The leaves are evergreen, renewing about every third year. They are a soft, gray-green in color, long and slender with a shimmering beauty. As Hosea 14:6 says: "His branches shall spread, and his beauty shall be as the olive tree ..." (KJV).

The flowers are cream-colored, with deeper yellow at the center. The small flowers are nearly hidden by the evergreen leaves. The trunk is gnarled and uneven. The wood is prized for making souvenirs for tourists. It is a beautifully veined, hard, and enduring wood and may be used for building furniture or cabinets. The trees are very long lived, 500 years or more. Some of the trees in Palestine may be as many as 2,000 years old.

The fruit is harvested for oil in the fall. The olives turn from green to black when ripe. Then long poles are used to knock the olives down. They are placed in a large stone oil press consisting of a large concave base, with a hole in the center upon which a large convex stone is placed and turned.

The Garden of Gethsemane, where Jesus spent his last night before Good Friday, literally means "garden with the olive press." Two other interesting biblical references are Judges and Romans. Judges 9:8-15 is the story of the trees choosing a king and asking the olive to reign over them. In Romans 11:16-25, Paul's allegory suggests that the Gentiles are the "wild olive" grafted to the "good olive" to which the Jews once belonged.

Lessons From The Olive

The olive branch has been a symbol of peace and goodwill in many cultures for thousands of years. Genesis 8:11 tells of Noah sending out a dove to see if the flood is over. The dove returns with an olive leaf, a reminder, as was the rainbow, that God had finished his punishment. God's continued goal would be peace and goodwill to all. As we keep our Christian light burning with the fuel God provides, we can help hold high our Lord Jesus as the Light of the World.

162

Prayer

Dear Lord Jesus, our Prince of Peace,
Let there be peace on earth,
And let it begin where we reach out to touch another life.
Let it begin where we accept people of other races, creeds,
    and colors
As members of our family.
Let it begin where Jews and Palestinians now are at war.
Let it begin where families have been verbally or physically
    abusive.
Yes, let there be peace on earth,
In such a wonderful way that the weapons of war will
    become
The implements of agriculture.

> *Peace, perfect peace, our future all unknown?*
> *Jesus we know, and he is on the throne.*
> *Peace, perfect peace, in this dark world of sin?*
> *The love of Jesus whispers peace within.*
> — E. H. Bickersteth

We pray in Jesus' name. Amen!

Scarlet

A Time For Purification

> *... then the priest shall pronounce the house clean, because the plague is healed. And he shall take to cleanse the house two birds, and cedar wood, and **scarlet**, and hyssop ... and he shall take the cedar wood, and the hyssop, and the **scarlet**, and the living bird, and dip them in the blood of the slain bird, and in the running water, and sprinkle the house seven times....*
> — Leviticus 14:48-49, 51 (KJV)

The word *scarlet* is used fifty times in the King James Version of the Bible. Usually it is used in reference to colors for the tent of meeting (Exodus chapter 25) or symbolically (Exodus chapters 17 and 18).

The plant we consider in this story is the source of the dye for scarlet. The text above tells how a house infected with the plague could be made clean using scarlet and other ingredients. Isaiah 1:18 (RSV) is a reminder of how the sin of humankind also can change from scarlet to pure white: "Come now, let us reason together, says the Lord; though your sins are like scarlet, they shall be as white as snow; though they are red like crimson, they shall become like wool."

The plant from which the scarlet then was derived is an evergreen shrub, classed as an oak, and growing as high as twenty feet. It is a native of the whole Mediterranean region. This plant has small thorny leaves which resemble a holly tree. In the fall season, half-inch acorns appear. These acorn cups have spreading spiny scales. The kermes insect (*Chermes ilicis*) breeds on the young shoots of this shrub. This insect is attracted to the soft, white down. It is the female insect which produces the beautiful scarlet dye.

It is interesting that two current dictionary references associate the color of scarlet with sin. They include: "flagrantly immoral" and "badge of adultery." Historically, if an unmarried woman had a child, or she was caught as an adulteress, she had to wear a scarlet letter *A* in public.

Scott Patton

One story of the Old Testament involving scarlet material tells how a prostitute helped some spies of the Children of Israel. Joshua 2 tells about the spies sent to Jericho who found refuge in the house of a prostitute named Rahab. She hid them from her own people with the assurance that when the people of Israel conquered Jericho, they would spare her home, her life, and her family's lives. The sign to save them would be a scarlet cord tied to the window. And that scarlet cord is what saved them.

The scriptures give evidence that Rahab changed her ways and became a true follower of God. She said, as recorded in Joshua 2:11: "The Lord your God is God in heaven above and here on earth." Rahab is even included in the roll call of the faithful, as recorded in Hebrews 11:31.

Lessons From Scarlet

While scarlet has some negative references, it was highly prized and valued as a part of the yarns for the tabernacle furnishings (Exodus 25:4; 26:1, 36, and following verses) and for vestments of the priests (Exodus 28:5-6 and following verses). Read some of the Bible references including all of Joshua 2. Scarlet came from the kermes insect that lives on the prickly oak. What other unique sources for dye are there?

Prayer

> Lord, my sins they are many, like the sands of the sea,
> But the blood, of my Savior, is sufficient for me;
> For thy promise is written in bright letters that glow,
> "Tho' your sins be as scarlet, I will make them like snow."
> Yes, my name's written there on the page white and fair;
> In the book of Thy kingdom, Yes, my name's written there.
>
> — Mary A. Kidder

Praise be to God! Amen!

Bay Tree

Laurels For A Baccalaureate

*Wait on the Lord, and keep his way, and he shall exalt thee to inherit the land ... I have seen the wicked in great power, and spreading himself like a green **bay tree**. Yet he passed away....*
— Psalm 37:34-36 (KJV)

At one time the luxuriant evergreen bay tree was very common in Palestine. It grew wild along the streams and moist valleys from the coast to the mountains. It is a handsome tree with majestic shiny leaves. One can understand why the Psalmist would use the proud bay tree as a symbol of the pride of the wicked. It is easy to imagine an old bay tree towering fifty feet into the air, indifferent to the troubles around it. The bay tree can symbolize a rich person utterly indifferent to the poverty and want of the common people. The only reference in the Bible is given above, and it is found only in the King James Version.

The bay tree has a fascinating story to tell. The bay belongs to the laurel family of trees and goes by the scientific name of *Laurus nobilis*, and is also known as Grecian laurel, or sweet bay. *Baccalaureate* literally means "laurel berry" or "crowned with laurel." Our term *poet laureate* has a similar background, reminding us of the distant days when people of distinction were honored by having their brows wreathed with sprigs of laurel or myrtle leaves.

Wearing sprigs for honor comes from Greek legend. Apollo, the Greek god of prophecy, was madly in love with a nymph named Daphne. Hiding from him, she turned herself into a bay tree. When he found out, he declared the bay tree sacred and wore a wreath of its leaves on his head. So a laurel of bay leaves was given to victors in battle and victors in sporting events, including the Olympics. A temple dedicated to Apollo at Delphi was thatched with boughs of bay leaves. This served as a sunscreen and also was believed to protect against lightning, disease, and evil spirits.

167

Scott Patton

168

Bay leaves were also used in infusions to aid in digestive disorders, and were applied to injured areas to ease sprains. Some, even today, find such treatments helpful. Bay leaves are presently available as an herb and are used effectively by many cooks. The attractive spear-shaped leaves and tempting aroma make bay branches a pleasing addition to floral arrangements. Many people who live where bay trees grow enjoy a walk among them, especially following a rain when the fragrance is delightful.

Bees love the abundant cream-colored waxy blossoms. When harvesting the leaves, care must be taken to avoid the cherry laurel, a decorative but poisonous tree. A sure test is to crinkle the leaves. The spicy fragrance released is a reliable method to identify the bay laurel.

Lessons From The Bay Tree

Psalm 37 has some treasured promises, not just a warning for the wicked. I have been spiritually lifted by:

> *Seek your happiness in the Lord, and he will give you*
> *your heart's desire. Give yourself to the Lord; trust*
> *in him, and he will help you....*
> *The Lord saves righteous men and protects them in times*
> *of trouble. He helps them and rescues them....*
> — Psalm 37:4-5, 39-40 (TEV)

Prayer

Lord Jesus, sometimes we turn aside from your humility because of the laurels or recognitions that may come our way. We have been guilty of pride like the pompous bay tree. We remember how you humbled yourself, becoming obedient to death, even death on the cross.

May we willingly accept a cross of service, sometimes even suffering, that you have for us to bear. Bless those who now serve you around the world, some of them facing severe suffering and the risk of imprisonment for acting out or speaking boldly of your love.

We pray in the name of Jesus our Lord and Savior. Amen!

Hyssop

Reaching For The Heights

Moses called for all the leaders of Israel and said to them, "Each of you is to choose a lamb or a young goat and kill it, so that your families can celebrate Passover. Take a sprig of **hyssop**, *dip it in the bowl containing the animal's blood, and wipe the blood on the door posts ... of your house. He ... will not let the Angel of Death enter your houses and kill you."*
— Exodus 12:21-23 (TEV)

... so a sponge was soaked in the wine, put on a stalk of **hyssop**, *and lifted up to his lips.* — John 19:29 (TEV)

Hyssop is a member of the mint family, a small bushy plant with attractive white to golden-colored flowers. At one time people used hyssop to season foods and as a medicine. If dipped in water, the many small stems and leaves hold the moisture well. The use of a "sprig of hyssop," as referred to in the scripture above, seems to have set the pattern for most of the other biblical references.

The cleansing of lepers included the use of hyssop:

Then shall the priest command to take for him that is to be cleansed two birds alive and clean, and cedar wood, and scarlet and hyssop.
— Leviticus 14:4, also vv. 6, 49, 51-52 (KJV)

As some scriptures suggest, the sap of the hyssop may have a cleansing quality. David, in Psalm 51:7, recognizes this purifying power: "Purge me with hyssop, and I shall be clean: wash me, and I shall be whiter than snow."

The theme of this story is "Reaching For The Heights." Even from the cross, Jesus directed us to the heights of heaven, but how could a sprig of hyssop reach to his lips? He had just spoken words of forgiveness even to those involved in the crucifixion.

The hyssop plant and branches are normally no longer than thirty inches. So how were they able to lift the wine to Jesus on the cross? There are several possibilities. One possibility is that an exceptionally long-stemmed hyssop plant may have been available. Another possibility is that both the sponge and the hyssop to support it could have been tied to a long reed or pole. Both Matthew and Mark refer to a reed, but also say that he did not drink from the sponge. I believe the sponge was offered to him twice. The first sponge contained gall, as a drug to lessen the pain, which Jesus refused. The second sponge contained cheap wine or vinegar, without gall, briefly quenching his parched mouth.

I fully agree with Mr. Barclay's analysis as told in his *Daily Study Bible Series: The Gospel of John* concerning whether or not hyssop could have been used at the cross:

> *It was hyssop which John wrote and hyssop which John meant ... It was the blood of the Passover Lamb which had saved the people of God; it was the blood of Jesus which was to save the world from sin. The very mention of hyssop would take the thoughts of any Jew back to the saving blood of the Passover lamb; and this was John's way of saying that Jesus was the great Passover Lamb of God whose death was to save the whole world from sin.*

Lessons From Hyssop

Some people wish they were taller. Despite its small size, the hyssop plant became a Passover symbol reminding people of being saved from death. It's also a symbol of cleansing, and most significantly, a conveyer to quench the thirst of Jesus in the darkest hour.

In our darkest hour we can turn to Jesus.

Prayer

Lord Jesus, we remember
The instructions by Moses
To place the blood of a lamb
Over the door post

So the angel of death
Would pass over.
When you were on the cross,
Hyssop was lifted to you.
It is your sacrifice
That delivers us
From the power of death.
Cleanse us, dear Lord,
And make us whole again.
Lead, enlighten, and empower us
With the presence and power of your Holy Spirit.
We pray in the name of Jesus,
Our suffering servant and Savior.
Amen!

Mustard

The Significance Of Small Beginnings

*He put before them another parable: "The kingdom of heaven is like a **mustard** seed that someone took and sowed in his field; it is the smallest of all the seeds, but when it has grown it is the greatest of shrubs and becomes a tree, so that the birds of the air come and make nests in its branches."*

— Matthew 13:31-32 (NRSV)

With just a quick reading of the verses above, it could seem like a drastic exaggeration with little value. While the black mustard has a tiny seed, there are other seeds that are even smaller. But it is true that the mustard plant in Palestine is larger than other garden shrubs and grows so quickly and large, that birds can rest in it, and even smaller birds might nest in it. William Barclay in his book, *Daily Study Bible Series: The Gospel of Matthew*, clarifies this:

> *The mustard plant of Palestine is very different from the mustard plant which we know in this country. To be strictly accurate the mustard seed is not the smallest of seeds ... but in the East is proverbial for smallness. For instance ... if they were talking of some small breach of the ceremonial law, they would speak of defilement as small as a mustard seed; and Jesus himself used the phrase in this way when he spoke of faith as a grain of mustard seed (Matthew 17:20). In Palestine this little grain of mustard seed did grow into something very like a tree.*

Jesus also talked about yeast, and the great power it has. With the parable of the mustard seed, we are reminded that small things can make big differences.

Just as one mustard seed can produce a large plant, one person can produce an abundance of good. A seldom remembered but

174

great story of Christian example is the story of a desert hermit by the name of Telemachus. He felt the call of God that he must go to Rome. By that time, Rome was nominally Christian, but still held gladiatorial games in which men fought each other to the death before huge, cheering crowds. Wondering what this was all about, Telemachus attended one. He was horrified to see such viciousness and cruelty. As the game was underway, Telemachus climbed into the arena and for a while disrupted the fight. The crowd yelled for him to leave, and threw stones at him. More than once he was knocked down, but he would not leave. Finally with a thumbs-down signal from the crowd and the emperor, a sword flashed, and Telemachus was dead. There was a great hush, and slowly the crowd left with an awareness that because of their game, a holy man lay dead. That was the beginning of the end of that savage form of recreation. One man walked a lonely walk and changed an empire.

The mustard plant is a colorful plant with large, ragged, dark green leaves and clear lemon yellow-colored flowers. Mustard for table use comes from the seeds. Some find it enhances meat and other dishes in a significant way. It also has been used to make poultices for external application as a cure for illnesses.

Lessons From Mustard

The mustard seed from Palestine is a tiny black seed much smaller than the larger seed we are familiar with here. Jesus reminds us that believing in the kingdom of God can start in a small way. One person with one idea can lead others to believe. And it can happen in your home or in your place of work.

Prayer

O God, we are so prone to worship bigness, prestige, and power. Teach us today the lesson of the mustard seed. Thank you for the many little things that have greatly influenced us: a kind word or a seed of hope or truth planted during our formative years. Guide our lives in such a way that we might sow the seeds of faith, love, and Christian influence among those around us. May we truly believe and follow you with the awareness that little things make big differences. In Jesus' name. Amen!

Myrtle

A Crown For Nobility

*"You will leave Babylon with joy; you will be lead out of the city in peace. The mountains and hills will burst into singing, and the trees will shout for joy. Cypress trees will grow where now there are briers; **myrtle** trees will come up in place of thorns. This will be a sign that will last forever, a reminder of what I, the Lord, have done."* — Isaiah 55:12-13 (TEV)

The above verse brings to mind one of the purposes of this book, in terms of learning lessons about praising God from nature: "the trees will shout for joy." This is similar to the way Maltbie Babcock puts it in "This Is My Father's World": "All nature sings and round me rings the music of the spheres ... The morning light, the lily white, declare their Maker's praise."

The myrtle is a very useful, colorful, and decorative plant. From it were made wreaths to crown nobility, poets, and victors in sports. It is an elegant, thornless, compact evergreen shrub, which reaches eighteen feet in height. The myrtle plant likely originated in Africa and Asia. It is found today in the entire Mediterranean area. It withstands drought well, and it must not freeze.

The myrtle is prized for its fragrant leaves. They are brilliant green in color, and when chopped, they emit a pleasant fragrance similar to that of the orange blossom. It bears delicate, creamy-white flowers with large golden stamens. Surprisingly, the flowers continue to bloom from June through September. The small oval, bluish-black berries are attractive to birds and have medicinal value. As a natural medicine myrtle has been used to relieve inflammation of the respiratory tract and for bronchitis. In the past and still some even today, the ground-up berries have been used as a spice. The fragrance of the flowers, ranked by many as more exquisite than the wild rose, is prized, and is often used in wedding bouquets. Today in Syria all parts of the plant are dried for perfume.

Myrtle branches were normally used as a part of the "Feast of the Tabernacles." The feast, a time of thanksgiving for the harvest, lasted for seven days. People made booths or little shelters as a part of their festive celebration for the harvest. The booths were covered with branches, including the very leafy and fragrant myrtle. The people were expected to live in the booths during the week.

Queen Esther's Hebrew name was "Hadassah," the feminine form of the Hebrew word for myrtle. See Esther 2:7. Other Bible references include Nehemiah 8:15; Isaiah 41:19; 55:13 and Zechariah 1:8, 10, and 11.

Lessons From Myrtle

In our Father's world there is beauty all around. To receive a crown of myrtle was a high honor and it provided a delightful fragrance. In contrast, Jesus wore a crown of thorns. Some day, by the grace of God, we will join in crowning him with many crowns.

Prayer

God of Creation, we stand amazed in the presence of much of your creative work. When we consider an apple tree, we find the beauty of the blossoms, the flavor of the fruit, and the usefulness of the wood to be priceless. Likewise, the gift of the myrtle tree combines shade, fragrance, beauty, and flavor.

Work out your purpose in our lives this day and every day. In the Creator's name we say, thank you. Amen!

179

Thistle

Curse Or Blessing?

*And to the man he said, "Because you have listened to the voice of your wife, and have eaten of the tree about which I commanded you, 'You shall not eat of it,' cursed is the ground because of you; in toil you shall eat of it all the days of your life; thorns and **thistles** it shall bring forth for you; and you shall eat the plants of the field."*
— Genesis 3:17-18 (NRSV)

When God asked Adam to leave the garden because of his disobedience, he was told, "Cursed is the ground because of you." And seemingly the thistles that grew were a part of the curse. In most ways thistles are a curse, causing pain to those who try to pull them. They can grow prolifically almost anywhere and sap up the water and nutrients crops need.

I remember well the aggravating task of cutting thistles from corn fields or from the pastures during the spring and summer when I was at home on the farm. No matter how often we cut them, the next year there was always an abundant supply. The large attractive, soft, purple blossoms have a distinct and unique beauty.

The King James Version of the Bible includes the word *thistle* or *thistles* eight times. Each suggests in some way that the thistle is not a good plant. On the other hand, current use indicates that the thistle can be a helpful plant. The best kind of seed for some birds is the thistle. It is a food highly prized by small birds, such as the goldfinch, the house finch, and others.

Another blessing that comes from thistles of several varieties is that they provide food for the painted lady (*Vanessa caradui*) butterfly. This butterfly is perhaps the most widespread and abundant in the world, partly because of the abundance of thistles that it depends on for food. This butterfly is very colorful with mostly orange and black on its upper body; while on the underside of its wings, the color is rosy pink with black and white patterns. Similar to the monarch butterfly, the painted lady migrates from Mexico to

Canada, and from North Africa to Finland. As many as 300 million butterflies may be in one migration.

Lessons From Thistle

Matthew 7:15-16, 20 (NRSV) in part says:

> *Beware of false prophets, who come to you in sheep's clothing but inwardly are ravenous wolves. You will know them by their fruits. Are grapes gathered from thorns, or figs from thistles?... Thus you will know them by their fruits.*

The thorny thistles are easy to identify. The beautiful, silky flower can be deceptive, but unless we can reach the nectar as the butterfly can, we will find thistles a painful part of nature.

Even in the worst conditions we can find beauty. Plants, as well as people, are known by their fruits.

Prayer

Lord, we pray that we will be known for producing good
   fruit.
When mud and trouble are all around us, give us a song.
The disobedience of Adam and Eve still haunts us.
We also are tempted to become as gods,
Doing things our way instead of yours.
We ask for your forgiveness and for the indwelling presence
   of the Holy Spirit
As our hope, guide, and strength.
Come, Holy Spirit, come. Come as the fire and burn ...
Come as the wind and refresh ...
Come as the water and cleanse.
Convict, convert, and consecrate our wills
To our great good, and to your greater glory.
We pray in Jesus' name. Amen!

Thorns

From King Of The Jews To King Of All

*Pilate wanted to please the crowd, so he set Barabbas
free for them. Then he had Jesus whipped and handed
him over to be crucified. The soldiers ... put a purple
robe on Jesus, made a crown of* **thorny** *branches, and
put it on his head. Then they began to salute him....*
— Mark 15:15, 17-18 (TEV)

Jesus rode into Jerusalem as a Servant King on Palm Sunday.
He should have been honored, saluted, and crowned as king. Instead, before the week was over, he was ridiculed, reviled, and
placed on the cross. Even that gave proof that he is King of Kings,
King of All! Instead of a crown, Jesus was given a wreath of thorns.
The plant from which this wreath was made is the background of
this story.

There are several thorn-bearing plants in Palestine, ranging from
the size of a rose bush to the height of a fifty-foot tree. Scholars
generally agree that the *Paliurus spina-christi* is the plant used to
make the wreath or crown of thorns. As a shrub, it grows from
three to nine feet tall. At that size it would have been easily acces-
sible to the soldiers.

The leathery leaves of the *Paliurus* are green, oval-shaped, and
pointed. Inconspicuous tiny white flowers appear in the spring. Later
they turn into red, capsular, winged fruit, dangerous to pick, but
suitable for birds.

The branches are armed with stiff and sharp spines. The long,
sharp, and recurved thorns can easily cause deep and festering
wounds.

The following is attributed to Bernard of Clairvaux:

O sacred Head, now wounded,
With grief and shame weighed down,
Now scornfully surrounded
With thorns, thine only crown:

183

Scott Patton

O sacred Head, what glory,
What bliss till now was thine!
Yet, though despised and gory,
I joy to call thee mine.
What language shall I borrow
To thank thee, dearest friend,
For this thy dying sorrow,
Thy pity without end?
Oh, make me thine forever,
And should I fainting be,
Lord, let me never, never
Outlive my love to thee.

Lessons From Thorns

We are all humbled and amazed to realize that Jesus could have called thousands of angels to save him from the cross. Peter tried to defend him, but Jesus said: "Don't you know that I could call on my Father for help, and at once he would send me more than twelve armies of angels?" Matthew 26:53 (TEV).

Have you ever been called on to suffer in the name of Jesus? If so, in what way?

Prayer

Gracious Lord Jesus, as we remember your sacrificial love, may we be more willing to sacrifice for you. As you willingly bore the cross and the pain and humiliation during your mock trial, may we willingly take up the crosses we may be called on to bear.

By the power of your Holy Spirit, strengthen and guide us to areas of sacrificial service every day. We pray in the name of the Lamb of God who takes away the sins of the world. Amen!

Wormwood

When The Stars Begin To Fall

*And the third angel sounded, and there fell a great star from heaven, burning as it were a lamp, and it fell upon the third part of the rivers, and upon the fountains of waters; and the name of the star is called **Wormwood**: and the third part of the waters became **wormwood**; and many men died of the waters, because they were made bitter.* — Revelation 8:10-11 (KJV)

Wormwood is referred to only nine times in the Bible, and each time in reference to bitterness. Some of the newer translations just use bitterness instead of wormwood.

One might think from the Revelation passage above, that wormwood is poisonous, but it is not. It is bitter enough to be noxious but not deadly. The wormwood that grows wild in Palestine is more bitter than others. In England the wormwood, or mugwort as it is known, is grown for seasoning and medicinal purposes. In some parts of Europe and North Africa, wormwood has an important commercial use, supplying an essential oil which is used in the manufacture of medicine, or for flavoring some wines.

The sagebrush-like plant has pinnatifid, silvery, silky leaves. There are numerous nodding flower heads, greenish-yellow in color, small, round, and button-like.

One passage that talks specifically about bitterness is in Deuteronomy 29:18 (KJV). It is a warning about the punishment for turning away from God:

Lest there should be among you man, or woman, or family, or tribe, whose heart turneth away this day from the Lord our God, to go and serve the gods of these nations; lest there should be among you a root that beareth gall and wormwood.

Jeremiah 23:15 (RSV) also gives a similar warning, this time directed to the unfaithful prophets who brought a false message:

> *Therefore thus says the Lord of hosts concerning the prophets: "Behold, I will feed them with wormwood, and give them poisoned water to drink; for from the prophets of Jerusalem ungodliness has gone forth into all the land."*

Lessons From Wormwood

The symbolic language of Revelation includes the blowing of seven trumpets by seven angels (Revelation 8:7 and following verses). Each brings some sort of terror or trouble. The first four seem to announce the releasing of the "Four Winds of the Lamb's Wrath" (Revelation 6:17—7:3). The sounding of the third trumpet announces the falling of a great burning star, that includes the wormwood reference. Some scholars believe these symbols stand for things that happened in the Roman Empire as the Huns and other enemies made a bloody slaughter of the Roman forces.

Prayer

> *O Lord, out of the depths I cry to you; now hear me calling.*
> *Incline your ear to my distress in spite of my rebelling.*
> *Do not regard my sinful deeds. Send me the grace my spirit needs;*
> *Without it I am nothing.*
> *All things you send are full of grace; you crown our lives with favor.*
> *All our good works are done in vain without our Lord and Savior.*
> *We praise the God who gives us faith and saves us from the grip of death;*
> *Our lives are in God's keeping.*
> *It is in God that we shall hope, and not in our own merit;*
> *We rest our fears in God's good Word and trust the Holy Spirit,*

Whose promise keeps us strong and sure; and sends
redemption through the Word.
Praise God for endless mercy.

— Martin Luther

Amen!

Index

Alphabetical List Of Plants